The Green School

How your school can achieve
and promote sustainability

Stan Terry

Adamson Publishing

Copyright © 2008 Stan Terry

Published by Adamson Publishing Ltd
8 The Moorings
Norwich NR3 3AX
01603 623336, fax 01603 624767
info@adamsonbooks.com
www.adamsonbooks.com

First published 2008

ISBN 9780-948543-47-0

British Library Cataloguing in Publication Data
A catalogue record for this book is available from the British Library

Cover design by Geoff Shirley
Edited by Stephen Adamson and Tim Cawkwell

This book has been printed on paper consisting of 80 percent recycled fibre.

Printed and bound in Great Britain by Biddles Limited, King's Lynn, Norfolk

Contents

1 Why Sustainability?

Congratulations! You have taken the first step to making your school sustainable by buying, borrowing, or simply starting to read this book.

"Sustainability", "sustainable development" and "education for sustainable development" are all buzzwords which have come into use over the last thirty years. They challenge our thinking about the way in which we use the Earth's resources, especially how we appear set on destroying the planet that supports us.

Competing theories exist about the impact humanity is having on the planet. The range and complexity of these theories is huge and getting a grasp on them can be a significant obstacle to getting started with the search for solutions. But one thing is certain, that the next fifty years will see many significant challenges for the youngsters who are in our schools today. Principal among them will be to revise our current model of development and remove the threat that the ever-increasing use of our natural resources places on the ability of future generations to survive.

As the environmental campaigner and Chairman of the UK Commission for Sustainable Development, Jonathon Porritt, has said:

> "For those of us closely involved in the sustainable development stakes, it's nail-biting stuff – even though this is a race being played out over decades rather than minutes. The stakes could hardly be higher: can we reach that point in our evolutionary history where we start to live sustainably on this planet before we inflict irreversible damage on the life-

support systems that sustain us? Or will we remain hell-bent
on testing those systems to destruction (and beyond)?"[1]

If we don't rethink the way in which we treat the planet we will
be creating the seeds of our own destruction. The world on which
we live has been transformed in the last seventy-five years by the
joint effects of increased economic expansion and rapid
population growth. Because of this combination more than one
half of the planet's original forest area has been lost in this period,
and more than a third of what's left will disappear in the next
twenty-five years. More than one third of the world's coral reefs
are already dead or significantly damaged. In the cultivated areas
of the world human activity has, according to the UN Food and
Agricultural Organization, resulted in the fertility of at least 20
per cent of the total cultivated area being seriously degraded. Air
quality has declined across the world, significantly increasing the
incidences of respiratory disease. The World Health Organization
(WHO) has estimated that some 800,000 people die prematurely
each year as a result of illnesses caused by air pollution. Despite
efforts to remove them, CFCs (chlorofluorocarbons) and other
ozone-depleting substances continue to be used in many developing parts of the world, damaging the thin skein of the atmos-
phere that protects us from solar radiation.

Concern is increasingly expressed about the quantity and quality
of fresh water available across the globe, despite significant efforts
by many countries to regulate the use of water resources as
dumping grounds for pollutant chemicals (Millennium Ecosystem
Assessment Report, 2005). The ability of ecosystems worldwide
to provide clean and reliable sources of water has been severely
impaired.

All in all, our demands for food, fresh water, and fuel have significantly impacted on the ecosystems of the planet in the last 75
years, contributing significantly to a largely irreversible loss in the
diversity of life. While a lot of humanity has enjoyed increased
levels of well-being and economic development, this has come at
a significant cost to ecosystems. It has also produced dispropor-
tionate inequalities between peoples and societies.

The capacity of the planet to overcome these degradations is becoming impaired. We have not as yet reached the "tipping point" of irretrievable damage but many scientists believe we are accelerating rapidly towards it. The outcome of doing nothing threatens our very presence, yet our species has no sacrosanct right to continue to exist. If we don't learn to live sustainably within natural systems, we will share the destiny of other life forms that failed to adapt. In other words, the same fate could await us as we have condemned other species to – extinction! Not in the next fifty to one hundred years but ultimately, unless we learn to live within constraints which will ensure our survival, that is to say, we learn to live sustainably.

The political reality at present is that although a lot of lip service is paid to the environment, protecting it takes a poor second place to increasing material prosperity. But achieving sustainability is the major political issue we have to face.

The UK government has stated clear goals: "To enable all people throughout the world to satisfy their basic needs and to enjoy a better quality of life without compromising the quality of life for future generations ... Government must promote a clear under-standing of, and commitment to, sustainable development so that people can contribute to the overall goal through their individual decisions. Similar objectives will inform our international endeavours, with the UK actively promoting multilateral and sustainable solutions to today's most pressing environmental, economic and social problems."[2]

Understanding the terms

The language of sustainability is often poorly understood by non-environmentalists so there is a need to identify what is meant by those terms we used at the beginning of this chapter:

Sustainability is the capacity for survival in the long term. Anything that can continue to be done indefinitely is sustainable, while something which cannot go on being done indefinitely is by definition unsustainable. Sustainability is an end goal.

Sustainable development is the process by which we as a

species move towards the end goal of sustainability.

Education for sustainable development (ESD) is the process of learning undertaken to make decisions that consider the long-term economy, ecology and equity of all communities.

The definition of sustainable development produced by the Brundtland report in 1987 is still probably the best to date: "Development which meets the needs of the present without compromising the ability of future generations to meet their own needs."[3] A narrow interpretation might suggest that this is about managing the environment more effectively. However, it is about social and economic issues as much as it is about environmental ones. To that end Brundtland is about ensuring that development occurs within a framework which understands that human well-being, even survival, is the ultimate goal.

By extension ESD is a process by which we educate the population (in this case our children) about sustainability. It enables people to develop the knowledge, values and skills to participate in decisions about the way we do things individually and collectively, both locally and globally, that will enhance our quality of life now, without damaging the planet for future generations. In the words of Tony Blair, writing in his then position as prime minister:

> "There is no magic wand that government or any one else can wave to make sustainable behaviour and activity the norm overnight. We will only succeed if we go with the grain of what individuals and businesses want, and channel their creativity to confront the environmental challenges we face. Development, growth, and prosperity need not and should not be in conflict with sustainability. This is a truly challenging agenda. It means focusing on long-term solutions." [4]

Why schools?

If we, as a species, are going to have to learn a new way of living in the future, where better to start than with today's young people?

This means educating the next generation now to understand

what they will need to do if they are indeed to achieve sustainability for our world. But this will not happen unless those involved in schools, especially school leadership teams and governors, first understand the agenda themselves and then look for ways to deliver it.

Jonathon Porritt has made the point that it is essential that schools not only talk about this agenda but are seen to practise what they preach – not just expounding the case for sustainability but living it by example. The message can then reach out to the wider community that this is about everyone's future.

In a consultation paper issued by the DfES in 2006, the government said that it would like every school to be a sustainable school.[5] According to this vision, every school should be seeking to integrate high standards of achievement and behaviour with goals for healthy living, community awareness, environmental awareness, a clear understanding of citizenship and global responsibility.

According to the DCSF (as the DfES became in 2007), a sustainable school should be one guided by the principles of care for oneself, care for others across time and cultures, and care for the environment. It is not just about the environment, but about how we organize our lives and our work. Hence it focuses on adopting a caring approach, to ourselves and to our communities as well as to the planet.

Sustainability is about finding solutions to improving the quality of peoples' lives across the world without storing up problems for future generations or creating additional problems for other peoples.

Leadership teams in schools set the framework by which the school moves forward. If sustainable development is to be successfully pursued within the nation's schools strong leadership will be needed.

As we will see, there is also a bonus for schools in this, since delivering the sustainable development agenda has been identified as producing significant improvements in student performance and attitudes. We will also see that research has shown that schools which follow an efficient sustainability agenda are also more cost-efficient.

However, the move to sustainable schools will not be easy. Schools are coming at this agenda from significantly differing starting points and face obstacles and objections. But they have been provided with a framework within which they can develop their own approach.

The DCSF has developed a system of eight "doorways" to help schools (see chapter 8) and has published a *National Framework for Sustainable Schools*. While these do not provide anything like all the answers, they do point schools in the right directions and help focus thinking.

School leadership teams can offer a vision of a more sustainable world to their students, the parents and their communities. After all, education should be at the heart of any truly transformative process.

References

1   Jonathan Porritt, *Progress: Sustainable Development Commission Annual Report 2004* Sustainable Development Commission, 2005
2   *Securing the Future – UK Government Sustainable Development Strategy*, Stationery Office, 2005
3   World Commission on Environment and Development, *Our Common Future* 1987
4   *Securing the Future*
5   *Sustainable Schools for Pupils, Communities and the Environment – a consultation paper* DFES, 2006

2 Testing Your Understanding

The first step on the way of getting your school to embrace the aims of sustainability is to gain understanding of the subject yourself. The following questionnaire is an opportunity to check your knowledge and understanding of the debate. Depending on your answers, you can then identify the implications for your school.

First answer the questions individually and then share your answers with colleagues or other governors prior to discussing the actions you need to take.

It would be a useful exercise to undertake this as part of a CPD opportunity in the school for the senior leadership team, including your governing body.

Carbon Emissions UK
1. Schools account for what percentage of carbon emissions from the public sector in the UK?

> *a. 5   b. 10   c. 15   d. 20   e. 25*

Energy efficiency
2. What percentage of UK schools have achieved the Building Research Energy Conservation Support Unit (BRECSU) good-practice benchmark for energy efficiency?

> *a. 25   b. 35   c. 45   d. 55   e. 65*

Climate Change Taxation

3. What is the Climate Change Levy? When was it brought into operation and what was its purpose?

4. What percentage is added to school energy bills by the Climate Change Levy?

> *a. 2   b. 5   c.7   d. 9   e. 10*

ICT and energy consumption

5. The average annual cost of energy consumption by secondary schools in the UK attributable to ICT is:

> *a. £12,350   b. £19,300   c. £22,400   d. £25,700*
> *e. £26,900*

6. What percentage of total energy consumption in UK schools is directly attributable to ICT use in schools?

> *a. 3   b. 5   c. 8   d. 10   e. 12*

Schools and waste

7. Waste produced by schools in England, Scotland and Wales in 2003/2004 amounted to how much?

> *a. 352,000 tonnes   b. 548,000 tonnes*
> *c. 661,000 tonnes   d. 725,000 tonnes*
> *e. 839,000 tonnes*

8. What percentage of schools' waste is presently consigned to landfill rather than recycled?

> *a. 28   b. 35   c. 47   d. 58   e. 72*

9. In 2003 what volume of construction waste was created in the UK?

> *a. 35 million tonnes   b. 55 million tonnes*
> *c. 78 million tonnes   d. 90 million tonnes*
> *e. 120 million tonnes*

10. What percentage of waste from UK schools is paper-based and therefore suitable for recycling?

> *a. 15   b. 45   c. 50   d. 58   e. 64*

Energy

11. The Energy Performance of Buildings Directive has applied to schools since October 2008. What does it require schools to do?

12. The average school could save how much, per pupil, by implementing simple energy-saving measures in its school sustainability plan?

> *a. £12.56   b. £15.47   c. £17.85   d. £19.23*
> *e. £20.17*

Air Quality

13. The School Premises Regulations 1999 specify that all occupied areas in a school building should have controllable ventilation at a minimum of 3 litres of fresh air per second for each of the maximum number of persons the area will accommodate. What percentage of primary school classrooms were found by the Building Research Establishment in 2001 to have failed to meet this standard?

> *a. 12   b. 37   c. 53   d.65   e. 68*

Water

14. What is the average school water bill for primary schools and secondary schools in the UK?

Primary

> *a. £850 p.a.   b. £1200 p.a.   c. £1350 p.a.   d. £1600 p.a.*
> *e. £1940 p.a.*

Secondary

> *a. £5500 p.a.   b. £8500 p.a.   c. £9300 p.a.*
> *d. £10,700 p.a.   e. £12,400 p.a.*

15. How much water does a constantly flushing urinal consume hourly?

> *a. 20 litres   b. 25 litres   c. 30 litres   d. 35 litres*
> *e. 40 litres*

16. How much did schools in England spend on water and treatment of waste water in 2003/4?

> *a. £50 million   b. £57 million   c. £63 million*
> *d. £72 million   e. £85 million*

Transport

17. How many million tonnes of CO_2 produced in the UK are directly attributable to the transport of children to schools by parents?

      a. 1.3   *b. 1.6*   *c. 1.9*   *d. 2.4*   *e. 3*

Resources

18. How much did schools in the maintained sector spend on furniture, teaching equipment and stationery in 2004?

      a. £900 million   *b. £1200 million*
      c. £1400 million   *d. £1500 million*
      e. £1800 million

19. What percentage of schools in 2005 have in place policies that identify the purchase of recycled materials for their school as a priority?

      a. 2   *b 8*   *c. 10*   *d. 12*   *e. 15*

20. In 2005 the Davis Langdon Consultancy identified, for the Waste Resources Action Programme (WRAP), that as much as 21 per cent of materials used in constructing new build schools under Building Schools for the Future could be recycled. What is the actual specified requirement?

      a. 5%   *b. 8%*   *c. 10%*   *d. 12%*   *e. 15%*

Answers

1. *15 per cent.*
Schools' total contribution to carbon emissions in the public sector in the UK includes the carbon emissions contained in the development of new buildings and the embodied energy contained within materials, as well as increasing amounts of CO_2 resulting from the development of extended schools and wrap-around provision (i.e. high-quality childcare combined with sports and arts activities, from 8am to 6pm). It is also evident that the amount of CO_2 attributable to the purchase of school materials and the transport miles incurred is increasing. Direct energy consumption is also growing significantly as a result of the greater use of ICT.

2. *25 per cent.*
The failure of most schools to achieve anything close to efficient use of energy is not just a symptom of poorly designed buildings but also of a failure to manage energy efficiently.

The majority of schools do little to monitor their use of energy on a daily basis. Few schools train their staff to consider energy utilization as part of their role. Very few teachers or support staff know the true cost of their consumption patterns.

3. *The Climate Change Levy was introduced in the UK in 1999 as part of the government's programme of measures to reduce energy consumption.*
In 1997 the UK government set itself a target of a 20 per cent CO_2 reduction from 1990 levels by 2010, which goes beyond the levels agreed in the Kyoto protocol of 1997. Unfortunately, while the measure was directed at high-end energy users and was meant to be revenue-neutral through National Insurance adjustments if reductions were achieved, schools were caught in its net. Up to 2005 the levy had contributed a saving of some 16.5 million tonnes of CO_2 and in that year Cambridge Econometrics predicted that by 2010 that it will have secured a reduction of 2.9 per cent in energy demand in the UK.

4. *The Climate Change Levy adds 5 per cent plus VAT to schools' and businesses' energy bills.*
As a result of the 2007 Budget, the Climate Change Levy is meant to increase in line with inflation and schools will continue to be taxed on that basis. The overall increase to schools in energy costs is between 8 and 10 per cent annually.

5. *£19,300. The total energy spend related to ICT in UK is approximately £100 million.*
Some forms of ICT will have a significant impact on school energy consumption (with the exception of extra-low voltage systems). Computers, whiteboards, projectors, and other devices in schools can use a significant amount of energy. A sustainable ICT strategy is one that balances energy consumption with teaching needs. It requires a careful analysis to be undertaken by senior leadership teams in schools when thinking about the purchase and installation of such equipment. It is also important that schools evaluate

the whole-life cost of equipment – also known as its TCO, Total Cost of Ownership.[1] (The TCO is the cost of hardware and software purchased plus the cost of technical support services plus the training requirements plus the energy costs of running the equipment.)

6. *5 per cent.*

7. *839,000 tonnes.*
Industry recognises that waste minimization has a triple impact. Schools generally do not monitor the volume of inputs into their system nor do they monitor or manage effectively their waste outputs. However, the physical mass of goods and services entering and leaving the average primary or secondary school is significant).

Basic input	Mass flow kg/pupil year
Energy	285
Water	4258
Inert material	504
Plastic and packaging	3
Wood	15
Paper	10
Food	85
Chemicals	6
Total	5166

Basic output	Mass flow kg/pupil year
Solid	80
Liquid	4306
Gas	280
Total	5166

The mass balance of a typical school[2]

Equally schools do not measure or identi
produce. Targets are rarely set for redu
and re-use of waste is rarely contempla
little planning has gone into understanc
the school.

The evidence from Waste Watch[3] is th
waste by weight produced by school
paper and cardboard. It found that the average w.... ,
per year is some 22 kg and that schools only recycle on average
32 per cent. The average amount of waste produced annually by
primary schools per site amounts to 6.1 tonnes and secondary
schools 14.3 tonnes.

8. *72 per cent.*

9. *90 million tonnes.*
Schools which are to be rebuilt or significantly refurbished under
the Building Schools for the Future programme (BSF) have a
particular responsibility to ensure that their building project
minimizes the waste created. They need to insist that architects
and contractors use a significant proportion of recycled materials
in the building and that the site has a policy of recycling all
materials, including separation of materials at source to ensure
minimal amounts are sent to landfill.

10. *50 per cent.*

11. *The Energy Performance of Buildings Directive has required
the energy rating of all schools to be assessed and displayed since
2008.*
Conducting a building survey to examine use of energy can
identify energy-saving measures that can be implemented as part
of the ongoing management of the buildings. Energy advice is
freely available to schools from the Centre for Research Education
and Training in Energy (CREATE) and energy audits can be
undertaken with support from the Carbon Trust or the Energy
Savings Trust to develop a systematic energy policy process. Many
of the measures which can help to reduce energy consumption are
at nil overall cost or have significant payback within two to three
years.

utput of schools can be reduced by 23 per cent by
nting energy-saving measures that include direct
om lighting controls, movement sensors, simple regular
ning of lights, and fitting fewer but more efficient fluorescent
bes.

13. *68 per cent.*
Air quality has been identified by the US Environmental
Protection Agency as a significant factor in teacher and student
performance. School buildings contain many pollutants, mainly
associated with decoration, furniture and the chemicals used in
cleaning. In a study of 16 UK schools undertaken by the Building
Research Establishment, CO_2 concentration levels in classrooms
indicated that more than half of all classrooms exceeded the daily
average of the level conducive to a healthy environment.

14. *Primary £1940, secondary £8500.*
The majority of schools do not undertake weekly analysis of their
water consumption, and few schools have any form of water-
saving measure. There is little awareness in schools of the environmental impact of water consumption. Average consumption
figures in the primary sector are approximately $7m^3$ per annum
per pupil and in the secondary sector $11m^3$. Significant financial
savings could be made by implementing water management
approaches and by fitting water-saving devices. The DCSF
estimates indicate that usage could be reduced to some $4m^3$ per
pupil in both primary and secondary schools, which could result
in savings in excess of £5000 per annum for a school of 600
students.

15. *25 litres per hour.*

16. *£72 million.*

17. *1.3 m tonnes.*
Research by the Department for Transport[4] has shown that one in
five vehicles on the road at peak traffic times is transporting a
child to school, and that 68 per cent of all journeys are of less than
5 miles. Bicycling to school has declined by 44 per cent since
1985-6.[5] Declining numbers of children make their own way to
school.

The impact of less exercise on school children is evident. 30 per cent of boys and 39 per cent of girls do not achieve recommended levels of physical activity in any week. 5 per cent of boys and 7.2 per cent of girls are clinically obese, while one in five boys and one in four girls is classified as officially overweight.

18. £1200 million.
Schools have significant purchasing power. They are often the biggest employer in a local community and if they used their purchasing power within their immediate community they could have a significant impact on local businesses. Local purchasing also means fewer CO_2 transport miles for the products they buy.

19. 2 per cent.
If schools had policy statements which identified the purchase of recycled materials and products as a school priority it would significantly stimulate the market place for such goods in the UK. The same is true of paper from environmentally sustainable or recycled sources.

20. 10 per cent.

Outcomes

17-20 correct You have a very good understanding of the reasons for being a sustainable school

12-16 correct You have good knowledge but there are some gaps. You probably realize that there is a lot to learn about sustainability.

7-12 correct You have some knowledge but there are major gaps in your understanding and you need as a team to develop your knowledge.

Below 7 correct You are just beginning to consider how your school should address sustainability.

Don't be downhearted if you did not get right answers to a lot of these questions, as they have been posed to encourage debate. If you did get a low score (or if you were just a lucky guesser!), then you should start a debate as to how the school can more effectively get to grips with the way in which it is sustainably managed.

Significant change will not happen if only a few people at the top go for it. Only a positive team approach will produce it. But leadership is still essential, as change in any organization needs to be understood and managed in a way that all people can cope effectively with. Changing to a sustainably focused approach to the management of the school cannot be imposed; people and teams within the school need to be empowered to find their own solutions and responses.

References

1   *Total Cost of Ownership (TCO) and Investment Planning* BECTA, 2005
2   *Resource Management in the Education Sector* BIFFA 2004
3   *Greening Britain's Schools: a study into the sustainability of our schools* Southampton Environment Centre and Maverick Energy, a Biffaward project 2001
4   *Attitudes to, and Potential Take-up of, Additional Home-to-School Transport* www.dft.gov.uk
5   See the Sustrans website, www.saferoutestoschools.org.uk

3   Your School's Environmental Impact

Fact 1

As we have seen in the previous chapter, schools are known to contribute some 15 per cent of all public sector CO_2 emissions in the UK.[1] That is equivalent to some 5 million tonnes of CO_2.

Fact 2

The DCSF has a target to reduce carbon emissions from schools by 10 per cent of 2000 levels by 2010 (or 20 per cent of 1990 levels by 2010) to reflect Kyoto targets. In addition the government is aiming for schools to be carbon-neutral by 2020. Schools need to be prepared to take on this challenge.

However, concern with their environmental impact has not been a priority for most schools. Certainly, until very recently, they have had little in the way of central direction on this issue from either the government or local authorities, for whom environmental management has lain outside the arena of education. But, quite apart from the urgency of environmental change, government action is set to change that.

Undoing neglect

While it is true that a lack of investment in preventative maintenance and in improving school buildings by government and local authorities throughout the 1980s and 1990s meant that there were systemic problems with capital funding for schools, schools did little to understand the environmental issue themselves. Not much effort was made to understand the environmental impact of school premises and there was understandably a greater emphasis on make do and mend, rather than understanding the need to evaluate the process.

Similarly, local authorities paid little regard to the environmental performance of school buildings and management practices. This may be largely due to a run-down of property services divisions in many local authorities in the 1990s, as identified by the National Audit Office (NAO) in 2003. However, since 1999 funding for capital projects and maintenance has increased substantially, and the opportunities for schools are now much better. With more responsibility devolved to them, they can now link building projects to their school development and improvement plans so as to be systematic in planning and monitoring how they spend their resources.

There has been significant investment by the government in recent years in the production of guidance materials for asset management, in best-practice events, and in seminars and training programmes designed to develop understanding among local authority officers and school leadership teams. At the same time the DCSF has sought to obtain improved data about building conditions. However, the information provided by schools and local authorities is still often flawed and unreliable, and is therefore not good enough to form the basis for serious planning.

This is compounded by what in 2003 the NAO identified as a lack of investment in skilled staff in property service departments. The same NAO report revealed that the majority of schools expressed concern about the lack of support from local authorities and their inability to "grasp the culture of meeting clients' needs".

But the problem is not only in local government. Schools need effective in-house expertise and technical skills if they are to be pro-active as clients for the building services they receive or purchase, but the evidence is that they have significantly differing levels of in-house skill, and many have seriously underestimated the knowledge and skills required. In 2000 the Audit

Commission[2] expressed concern about the ways schools linked priorities to resources and about their limited strategies for evaluating the impact of their spending decisions. It made it clear that schools need to secure good quality technical support to meet their responsibilities. In many cases that will mean getting it from outside.

This does not mean acquiring a builder's skills, but a client's. It is a matter of understanding the effective management of buildings and resources, and, in terms of caring for the environment, learning how to manage both present and future buildings and grounds in a sustainable way.

This requirement will become ever more important as the Building Schools for the Future programme proceeds to invest some £46 billion in renewing the education infrastructure of England over the next ten years.

But an attitude of "can't do" or "too expensive" is still widespread. This can be attributed to a number of common misunderstandings (see overleaf).

Energy consumption in schools

According to the Building Research Establishment[3] energy costs in schools are:

For primary schools	an average of £6300 p.a.
For secondary schools	dependent upon school size, on average between £39,000 and £55,000 p.a.

In total some £350–£400 million p.a. (2007 figures) is spent in the UK on heating and powering school buildings. One school can spend up to four times as much per pupil in energy costs as a similar school. This cannot be put down solely to the inefficiency of particular buildings.

Moreover, the trend is for costs to rise because the government's commitment to every school providing extended services can only increase energy consumption. If large numbers of schools become fully fledged "learning centres" for their communities, with

Energy myths

Myth *Energy is not a major budget item for most schools.*

Reality Energy costs are second only to staff costs and exceed the cost of supplies and books.

Myth *Schools cannot save much by being energy smart.*

Reality Changing habits can save significantly. Savings of several thousands of pounds a year are possible.

Myth *Energy efficiency is not related to student performance.*

Reality Evidence from the Heschong Mahone Group (1999 and 2003), an American consultancy on building efficiency, indicates that improved use of natural daylight and a consequent reduction in artificial lighting can have a significant improvement on student performance.

Myth *Energy improvements in existing buildings require major financial outlay.*

Reality There are government grants and lots of free advice around to enable schools to access the knowledge required.

Myth *Tracking energy use is unnecessary.*

Reality Tracking energy use helps schools identify waste and equipment problems as well as overcharging and errors on bills. Overcharging or incorrect billing is commonplace in the UK.[4]

Myth *All new buildings are energy efficient.*

Reality Unfortunately, this is not the case. Unless a school directs its architect to design energy-efficient buildings, new schools may be as inefficient as old ones. Or they may incorporate only modest energy efficiency measures.

Schools often focus on short-term construction costs instead of long-term, life-cycle savings. The key to getting an energy-smart and well-designed school is to ask for an energy-efficient design. If you don't ask, you don't get!

attached health, legal and social work facilities and open 52 weeks of the year, the increase in energy costs could be 50 per cent.

The challenge for schools will not just be environmental. With volatility in energy supply long-term budgeting will become very difficult.

In 2002 a report from the Sustainable Development Commission[5] made it clear that government should set clear and unequivocal targets for reduction in energy demand for all sectors of the UK, including education. However, the Energy Savings Trust[6] showed in 2005 that, far from reducing their demand, schools are in fact substantially increasing their energy use.

It need not be this way!

It has been estimated in the Energy Saving Consumption Guide 73, *Best Practice Programme*, by the Energy Technology Support Unit (ETSU) that savings of 5–10 per cent could be made across the schools' sector with little or no cost to schools, and indeed the Audit Commission believes that 10 per cent reductions could be easily achieved. This could save over £20 million a year and reduce indirect CO_2 output from schools by 300,000 tonnes per annum. Clearly the level of reductions possible is linked to the amount of work that schools put into monitoring and changing their consumption patterns. To achieve significant reductions will require the school management to undertake a careful evaluation of the ways in which they manage energy at present and identify ways in which they can reduce their overall demand.

Many schools, possibly including yours, have no idea about their real energy consumption patterns. They often rely upon historical bill costs, which in themselves have often been based on historically estimated amounts. The result is no real control of energy costs or consumption!

Making a start

1. Find all of your school meters. There may be different electricity meters for different tariffs.

2. Allocate regular reading of the meters to a named individual, or

---

Questions all leadership groups in schools should ask about their energy usage

Does our school monitor its use of energy?

Do we know where the electricity meters are to be found?

Do we read our meters regularly?

Does our school check that its fuel bills are correct when authorizing payment?

Does our school measure changes in consumption when new plant is installed (e.g. a new computer suite)?

Does our school establish typical weekly, monthly, and termly analyses of its energy consumption so that it can spot abnormal consumption patterns?

Does our school have sub-meters to measure consumption in the school kitchens? If not, why not? (School kitchens are major consumers of energy if they are not separately metered and monitored. Custom and practice in many school kitchens is energy inefficient.)

Does our school check that its spending is consistent with its budget allocation?

Does our school seek advice annually on best value for energy from an organization such as the Office for Government Commerce?

Does our school have someone with responsibility for monitoring and managing energy use?

---

engage pupils in the task. Or install half-hourly smart metering. Smart meters calculate energy consumption/costs and allow at-a-glance analysis of spending on energy. By taking half-hourly meter readings and by reducing billing errors and providing accurate bills, costs are managed more efficiently.

3. Check whether the meter references on your school bills correspond to the meters in your school. You might be surprised how often this is not the case.

4. Take meter readings at the end and the beginning of the school day. There may be a significant overnight difference. Can you account easily for it?

5. Identify equipment that appears to be left on standby during the school day. Ask whether it needs to be. If not ensure that it is switched off.

6. Ensure that lights are only switched on when they are needed.

7. Train all staff to institute a policy of switching off lights when not required or install movement or light sensors in each classroom which will progressively switch off banks of lights.

8. Ensure that all PC monitors and computer work stations are switched off when not in use, not left in standby mode. If necessary install technology that will power down all machines if left on.

9. Check your classroom and other space thermostat settings. Are they correctly set and do you check and compare with actual space temperatures?

10. Check whether your timing controls are optimized. If not adjust them regularly.

Following these actions should give you a considerable saving in overall energy costs.

Lighting

Lighting accounts for some 28 per cent of energy costs in schools. While lighting should provide appropriate luminance, ensure visual comfort and be energy efficient, good housekeeping can save a lot.

Lighting requirements for schools are covered by the School Premises Regulations[7]: "The maintained illuminance of teaching accommodation shall not be less than 300 lux on the working plane. In teaching accommodation where visually demanding tasks are carried out provision shall be made for a maintained illuminance of not less than 500 lux on the working plane." (Note: illuminance is the light level provided on a surface either by daylight or electric light.)

Even in winter there should be enough daylight in most of the school day to reach these levels without electric lighting. But research by the Lighting Research Centre at Rensselaer Polytechnic Institute in 2006 has discovered that in the majority of schools, once turned on lights are rarely turned off. It is good housekeeping for lights in classrooms to be switched off and only turned on if daylight levels fall.

One reason people leave fluorescent lights on is the belief that they use more energy if they are switched on and off frequently. That is not the case! If a room is going to be unoccupied for more than five minutes, switch off the lights.

There are other ways to save energy on lighting:

Savings of some 3 per cent can be made from **switching off** lights at break, lunchtime and after school.

Automatic lighting controls can save a further 5 per cent of a school's energy bill, with a payback period of some two years if they are fitted after the initial installation of equipment.

A regular **maintenance schedule** can also contribute to better lighting levels and also energy savings.

A regular **cleaning programme** of luminaires and reflectors will ensure that lighting levels in classrooms are efficient and may thus allow the switching off of banks of lights in classrooms. A dirty diffuser or luminaire can reduce lighting output by as much as 20 per cent.

Replacement of lighting is an opportunity for managers to consider more efficient luminaires and lamp types.

Significant saving can be achieved through **zoning** of lights, or controlling lights in groups for efficiency. Zoning allows lights to be switched on and off in rows.

Lights might not be needed next to a **window**, in which case their tubes can be removed.

Best of all, by making efficient use of **daylight** in classrooms, you can save an estimated 19 per cent on lighting costs. In designing a new building this should be a priority.

All tungsten light bulbs should be replaced with compact fluorescent lamps, which will save some 75 per cent of energy costs and will last far longer.

All 38mm fluorescent tube fittings should be replaced with 26mm triphosphor fluorescent tubes of a lower wattage (T5s and T8s – see chapter 5). Do this as 38mm tubes reach the end of their life and are being replaced as part of the regular maintenance process.

Fluorescent fittings with opal diffusers which are discoloured should be replaced. Whilst not saving energy, replacements provide some 30–60 per cent better lighting conditions.

Finally, get students involved to monitor light usage and run awareness campaigns amongst the student body.

Information and Communications Technology

Energy consumption by ICT equipment in schools can result in bills that are a lot higher than they need be, if not managed effectively.

The British Educational Technology Association (BECTA) has calculated that for secondary schools ICT requirements cost schools, on average, £19,500 p.a. in energy costs. It's a good policy to power down computers at the end of the morning and afternoon sessions – in other words, switch them OFF!

Is there an explicit environmental focus in your school's **purchasing policy**? When making purchases do you select only the most energy-efficient machines? For example, gas plasma screens consume about 20 per cent less energy than CRT technology.

There are significant differences too in the energy efficiency of desktop machines. For example, the Dell Dimension XPS 400 uses 258 watts per hour, while the same company's Dimension B110 uses 112 watts per hour. It is also important when buying machines to consider the whole-life costing of the purchases, which will include their energy consumption costs over their projected lifetime.

Alternatively, look at ICT solutions such as "Thin Client" technology. A **Thin Client**, sometimes called a Lean Client, is a low-cost, centrally managed computer devoid of CD-ROM players, diskette drives, and expansion slots, which runs all an organization's software from a server or remote site. They are designed to cost less in energy terms than PCs to run, consuming up to 85 per cent less energy than standard PC platforms. The Fraunhofer Institute for Applied Information Technology in Germany (2007) estimates that Thin Client saves 51 per cent of energy on average compared with traditional set-ups, with, of course, similar reductions in CO_2 production.

Another consideration is the heat created by running desktop PCs. Think of each of your PCs as a 150 watt light bulb, in terms of heat generated. Many schools now install air conditioning plant to cool their ICT rooms. This expensive and energy-hungry solution can be eliminated by employing a Thin Client system, saving the school even further on its energy costs and CO_2 figures.

Are your **printers** humming away unused? They usually incorporate a power-down option. Check to see if your IT technician has configured it on yours, and if not get it done.

It is also a good idea to incorporate time switches on printers and **photocopiers** in the school so that they are automatically switched off at night, at weekends and during school holidays, thus eliminating human forgetfulness.

Do the school's desktop **monitors** provide a cosy glow for the school's ghosts at night? Monitors are commonly left on at the end of the day, but even so-called power-saving options can consume up to 90 per cent of the power they would consume if the monitor was in use. Screen savers are not a low-power mode; in fact, complex ones can use more power than when someone is using the machine! Switching off monitors can save around 56 per cent of their operating costs annually.

Are your **PCs** acting as radiators? As we have just seen, each PC generates lots of heat. If the Basic Input/Output System (BIOS), which tells a computer what it can do without accessing programs from the hard disk, is configurable, get your IT technical support to adjust it to automatically manage power consumption of the PC. It does this by sending the hardware parts of the system into a "sleep mode", thus reducing significantly the power consumption of the PC. But standby modes still use power, in a range from 30 to 130 watts per hour dependent upon machine type. Switching computers off when not in use can save the school very large amounts of energy (between 100 and 400 kilowatts per computer per annum, depending on the model) and consequently several thousand pounds a year across a large network. That does not just mean at the end of the day but at lunchtime too. Getting pupils to do this will instil good habits.

Heating

The median energy cost per pupil for schools in England in 2003 was:

£25.76 for nursery schools

£24.23 for primary schools

£32.40 for secondary schools (Energy and Water Benchmarks from the DfES for maintained schools in 2002-03).

Heating and hot water make up 60 per cent of a school's energy budget.

Schools often set much higher classroom temperatures than they need to. The School Premises Regulations only require modest minimum temperatures:

18°C for parts of the school where there is a normal level of activity

21°C for areas where the occupants are inactive or sick

15°C for other teaching accommodation, such as washrooms, sleeping accommodation and circulation areas.

Turning up the thermostat by 1°C will increase your energy costs by 8 per cent.

Why set temperatures well in excess of these standards?

Certainly, children should not suffer uncomfortably cold or draughty areas, but if there are some, find out the cause and fix the problem rather than reaching for the thermostat. This is best undertaken by a walk around the buildings both inside and outside normal hours, looking for instances of wasteful use of energy and with a view to identifying opportunities for savings. It also provides a visible sign that you are committed to energy savings.

When were your **boilers** last serviced? Heating costs can increase by up to 30 per cent if a boiler is poorly operated or maintained. It should therefore be serviced annually and adjusted for optimum efficiency. This may involve investing in CPD for your site-management team.

The temperature of a whole building does not have to be set in one place. Programmable **thermostats** can be set to turn off heating in areas that are not in use throughout the day, such as those for circulation and cafeterias, and only provide heat when required.

Considerable savings can be made by some simple measures:

Encourage staff to keep classroom **doors** closed.

Look for **draughts** and seal them.

Make sure **thermostats** are positioned away from particularly hot or cold places, such as draughts, direct sunlight or sources of heat such as photocopiers.

Check that thermostats are operating correctly. If not clean them and if required replace them.

Install **thermostatic radiator valves** and check their settings regularly, or fit tamper-proof valves.

Ascertain whether all areas of the school have the same heating requirements (see above) and make certain that thermostat **settings** are appropriate and checked regularly.

Insulate all hot water tanks, boilers, valves and pipe work, particularly if there are long runs of it.

Consider installing **point-of-supply water heaters** where small quantities of hot water are required a long way from the main heating plant.

The Carbon Trust estimates that some 90 per cent of all building control systems, including those in schools, are inadequate. Good control of building services (heating, ventilation, cooling and lighting) not only saves energy and money, but produces a comfortable environment for staff and students.

Energy controls

Significant energy savings can be achieved simply by installing controls for lighting and heating. Of course, once installed, they need to be set, operated and maintained correctly. Usually some sort of time control is the most effective, depending on the occupancy pattern of the building:

Seven-day controls can best suit a school building that has varied use, as you can set for power to be off at weekends, say.

Optimum time controls can offer some 10 per cent efficiency over seven-day controls.

Boost controls adjust timings without over-riding existing controls. They can help to prevent heating systems being left on unnecessarily.

Make certain that pre-occupancy heat times are kept to a minimum. Check all temperature control settings regularly – preferably daily.

Occupancy controls, which give automatic control of lighting, heating and cooling within intermittently occupied areas of the building, can also be fitted. They are generally only useful for items such as lighting and individual ventilation fans that require a fast response. These detectors can be:

Passive infra red (PIR) – responding to body heat, and only "seeing" in direct line of sight

Ultra-sonic – emitting and receiving high-frequency sound waves so as to pick up small degrees of movement in a room

Microwave – providing good directional and spatial coverage, often used on doors

Hybrid – combining some or all of the above, and therefore more expensive.

Fact: most occupancy controls can pay back their initial cost within two years, in energy-saving terms. They can save you up to 15 per cent of your energy/heating costs.

Other controls can be incorporated which react to temperature and lighting levels.

The Carbon Trust has a site devoted to benchmarking schools' energy performance: http://217.10.129.104/energy_bench-marking/schools/default.asp.

Ask your management team how frequently they undertake any kind of energy monitoring. Perhaps more importantly, how much investment do they make in ensuring your services team are kept up to date?

Water

UK schools spend over £70 million per annum on water and waste-water treatment.[8] The average cost per school is some £2500 p.a., but large secondary schools can spend as much as £20,000 a year. Yet a carefully managed school may consume only half the volume of one of the same size that is poorly managed. As Wessex Water concluded after a survey of schools in 2006, there is a general lack of knowledge in schools as to the cost of their water consumption and the possible financial savings that can be achieved by effective management.

Water charges in schools are broken down into several elements, usually per cubic metre of water used plus a standing charge. There are separate charges for supply and sewerage services. Standing charges vary according to the size of the meter, and meter size in a school depends on the anticipated water consumption when the school was designed. As a result a school may have a meter that is oversized for its current usage, and should have a smaller one fitted. If you think this might be the case in your school, contact your water supplier or your local authority estate management service to check.

Another thing to check is whether the **fire-fighting supply** main passes through the school meter, which is often the case in older schools. It should bypass the school meter as it is exempt from charge, but if it does pass through the school main, then the main will be much larger than required by the size of school, and the school will be paying appropriately. Significant cost savings can be made by having it changed.

Do you analyse **water use**? Most schools don't. To undertake an analysis you need to have the annual consumption figure based on floor area or number of pupils. This should be expressed in litres per square metre or litres per person per annum. You can then benchmark your school performance against consumption in similar schools, as the Office for Government Commerce has established benchmark figures for schools in England, based on an analysis of 14,330 schools:

Primary school with pool – 4.3 m^3/pupil/annum

Primary school without pool – 3.8 m^3/pupil/annum

Secondary school with pool – 5.1 m^3/pupil/annum

Secondary school without pool – 3.9 m^3/pupil/annum.

The "best practice" benchmarks for schools are as follows:

Primary school with pool – 3.1 m^3/pupil/annum

Primary school without pool – 2.7 m^3/pupil/annum

Secondary school with pool – 3.6 m^3/pupil/annum

Secondary school without pool – 2.7 m^3/pupil/annum.

If your consumption figures are significantly higher than the relevant benchmark you need to ask why. And you then need to undertake an evaluation and implement volume- and cost-saving measures.

These figures indicate that a school could save approximately 30 per cent of its annual water costs. Across all the schools within the UK that would make a saving of 17,500,000 cubic metres of water. But to make these savings effective management processes need to be in place and be maintained.

Billing errors

The Office for Government Commerce (OGC) discovered in 2003 that 2 per cent of bills in a sample of organizations were incorrect. A number of different types of billing error were found:

wrong tariffs applied

wrong account number and site name

incorrect totals

meter readings that do not follow on from previous readings

duplicate bills

rateable values incorrectly levied

incorrect standing charges applied.

Schools are not exempt from these errors and may therefore be paying much more than they ought to. Don't just accept your water bills but scrutinise them to check for mistakes.

In general water is a "forgotten utility". But saving it is relatively straightforward. A small investment can save a school 15 – 20 per cent of its water bills annually. Such investments usually have a payback within 12 months or at worst 24, with the result that after that time financial savings can be considerable.

All public bodies now have a statutory duty, contained within Section 83 of the Water Act 2003, to take into account, where relevant, the desirability of conserving water.

The steps you can take as an organization are quite simple:

Locate your meter and read it weekly at least. It may be worthwhile initially to undertake a **daily analysis** of consumption.

To check for **leaks** turn off the stop taps in the school. If the meter is stationary there are no leaks, if the meter continues to run you may have a leak.

Read your bills to check for abnormal consumption.

Check your urinals. Are they fitted with **water-efficient controls**? Fitting passive infra-red controls can save as much as 60 per cent of your total water use and pay for itself within a year.

Check **cisterns** are operating at correct levels. Fit cistern displacement bags to reduce volumes of water used.

Check **taps** regularly. Are they dripping? As a first step renew all washers and then look to fit self-closing taps or spray taps with built-in flow restrictors.

Refit **plugs** where they are missing to reduce volumes of running water.

Push-button controls and time mechanisms on showers can significantly reduce waste. Fitting low-flow showerheads can also reduce water volumes considerably.

If long runs of exposed **pipe work** to showers and taps is the norm consider using point-of-use water heaters or ensure pipe work is lagged efficiently to discourage heat loss and consequent run-off.

Catering facilities on school premises need to be considered carefully and when replacing appliances more efficient models should be purchased.

Make staff and students aware of the need to **conserve** water. Encourage students to offer suggestions on water conservation.

On new-build facilities look to install **grey-water recycling** for washrooms. (Grey water is waste water generated from domestic processes such as dish-washing, laundry and bathing.)

Evidence from the National Clearing House for Educational Facilities in the USA[9] suggests that designing in water-efficiency measures can result in some 20–40 per cent reduction of costs for water and waste water.

This kind of reduction has substantial benefits to society, from reduced pollution to reduced infrastructure costs, by sending less water into the sewerage systems.

Even in a relatively wet place like the British Isles water costs are only likely to increase for the foreseeable future. Reducing the volumes will therefore result in considerable savings for the school, which can be re-invested elsewhere. This could amount to several thousand pounds per year.

Waste management

DEFRA have made clear in *Waste Strategy* (2007) that schools and young people have a "vital role in securing the future of our planet". Schools, DEFRA concludes, should become models of sustainable good practice. Its research into local-authority schemes to reduce waste and improve recycling found that the most successful ones involved schools and community groups. That said, schools are not, as yet, particularly successful exemplars of efficiency when it comes to managing their waste output.

According to Waste Watch, the UK produces at present some 38 million tones of waste materials from homes, offices and schools and approximately 72 per cent of school-derived wastes ends up in landfill[10], while the education sector as a whole produces some 700,000 tonnes of waste annually. At present most schools spend between £350 and £1000 p.a. on waste disposal.

Good environmental management relies upon practice being integrated into the structure of the organization. Evidence from the same study indicates that fewer than 25 per cent of schools give staff any form of environmental training, even though such training has been shown to have a significant impact on waste output in organizations. Yet at the same time some 84 per cent of schools carry out awareness-raising work with their students.

What does your school do?

Strategies to reduce waste and improve recycling in schools

Seek to reduce waste materials at source, i.e. at the procurement point. The products an organization purchases are a reflection of its commitment to sustainable development. The scale of purchasing within the sector means that there could be significant improvement in sustainability if the sector as a whole took this route.

The UK government's Sustainable Development Strategy (2005) commits the public sector to leading by example in delivering sustainable development objectives. That requires a step change in procurement practice. Schools, which are free to spend their devolved funding in any way that they choose, can influence suppliers by the way they purchase. They could, for example, work with them to increase the volume of sustainable procurement, prioritizing products with a recycled content. But changing behaviour – and in particular motivating sustainable behaviour – is far from straightforward, since individual patterns of behaviour are deeply embedded in social and institutional contexts. We are often guided as much by what others around us do and say and by the historical "rules of the game" as we are by personal choice.

Thus quite often schools are locked into purchasing unsustainably despite the best intentions being expressed by leadership teams. This occurs partly because of the infrastructure or because of apparently restricted choice, but it most often flows from habits, routines and dominant values. Thus a degree of habit enters behaviour, which then becomes difficult to change. Yet the decisions that organizations and individuals make to consume certain products and services all have direct and indirect impacts on the environment. What school leaders often lack when it comes to sustainable procurement is information about the available options.

Working with suppliers to reduce or take back packaging of products would make a considerable dent in the volume of waste materials that schools have to dispose of. A radical solution might be to refuse to accept any packaging of materials, by having in place a process whereby all deliveries are unpacked immediately and surplus packaging returned with the driver.

Being practical about recycling

Setting aside a space in the school grounds to serve as a community recycling hub, in conjunction with the local council, would emphasize the importance a school gives to recycling. It would help the council increase their recycling levels and ensure that the community receives the message that recycling is important to the school. It can also produce an income in the form of payment for the recyclable materials. Has your school spoken with the local council, or the council waste contractor, about such a scheme?

Separating waste materials at source goes a long way to improving recycling rates.

It is always important to keep in mind that by implementing an effective "reduce, re-use and recycle" programme significant financial savings can be made, often as much as 50 per cent of annual waste disposal costs.

However, a recent DCSF (2006) survey found that only 18 per cent of schools felt they were doing reasonable well with regard to waste reduction and recycling.

Get to grips with the paper waste produced by your school by:

> providing **scrap paper trays** in all classrooms
>
> ensuring that all photocopiers and printers are automatically set to **double-sided printing**
>
> setting up a system in the school for daily **collection of waste paper** for recycling
>
> providing parents with the opportunity to receive school **newsletters electronically** instead of in paper form
>
> looking for products that include **recycled content** when making purchasing decisions.

If your school still has drink-vending machines, ensure that all cans are recycled and make certain that the machine has a timer which switches it off when not in use during evenings, weekends and school holidays.

Set up a system to recycle printer cartridges and mobile phones in the school.

Set up a composting scheme for food waste by providing separate collection bins in the school canteen and around the school premises for the collection of compostable materials. You will need to educate children in what is and is not compostable. This can reduce the food waste leaving the school premises by as much as 50 per cent.

Food

The overriding aim of sustainable procurement is to drive sustainable consumption and the production of goods and services in order to achieve more with less while at the same time ensuring minimal environmental impact.

In schools, benefits from the sustainable procurement of food are likely to be:

a reduction in food miles

reductions in packaging and processing by increasing the proportion of fresh food in school menus

improvements to health in the school community by providing increased nutritional value in the food supplied.

In economic terms, sustainable procurement policies by schools and local authorities are likely to:

strengthen the local economy

increase local employment

provide support for local producers.

But as a study from Cardiff University points out[11], there is still a significant gap between the rhetoric of sustainable food procurement and the reality. That should not prevent leadership teams in schools promoting enlightened consumer behaviour among their students, seeking to embed the educational value of sustainably sourced school meals.

But that requires schools to think differently about their catering provision and not simply in terms of "best value" in its narrowest, i.e. cheapest, sense.

The last 50 years have seen dramatic changes in the food production and supply chain in the UK. This has come about because of:

globalization of the food industry, with an increase in both the import and export of food and wider sourcing of food within the UK and overseas

a concentration of the food supply base into fewer, larger suppliers, partly to meet perceived demand for bulk year-round supply of uniform produce

major changes in delivery patterns with most goods now routed through supermarket regional distribution centres, and a trend towards use of larger vehicles

centralization and concentration of sales in supermarkets, with a switch from frequent food shopping (on foot) at small local shops to weekly shopping by car at large out-of-town supermarkets.

The result has been significant increases in food miles from farm to consumer, with concomitant increases in air pollution, traffic congestion, accidents and noise. According to a 2005 study by DEFRA[12], food transportation accounts for some 25 per cent of all journeys by heavy goods vehicles (HGVs) in the UK. Further, such movements produce some 19 million tonnes of CO_2 (2002) while the direct economic, social and environmental costs amount to some £9 billion per year.

The total costs are significant compared with the gross added value of the agricultural sector. The report identifies that overall, lower food miles could strengthen local economies and communities, building closer links between consumers and producers. There would also be an additional spin-off of reduced packaging and its associated waste.

This would appear to be a win/win situation for schools in their food procurement strategies. By opening up contracts to local food suppliers local economies will be supported, but more importantly clear health and environmental benefits have been identified which will have long-term benefits for all. However, the evidence from the School Food Trust (2006) is that there is no quick fix. Overall there had been a reduction of an average 2.6 per cent in student numbers eating school meals in some local authorities since the drive to healthy school dinners, although in others demand had increased, with significant variation between local authority areas and also between primary and secondary schools. The best practice identified by the report indicates that the most successful implementation of such approaches is when schools develop "whole-school food and nutrition policies", which create opportunities for children to learn about food and nutrition while also learning about sustainable production.

In summary, if the leadership teams in schools do not in effect exemplify sustainable behaviour to their students and the community at large, by the ways in which they manage their organizations, then a significant opportunity to encourage major behaviour change will have been lost.

References

1   *Schools Carbon Footprinting Scoping Study – Final Report* Sustainable Development Commission, 2006
2   Audit Commission's report *Money Matters: School funding and resource management* 2000
3   *Review of Opportunities for Improved Carbon Savings from Spend on Education Buildings* (report for the Sustainable Development Commission, 2006)
4   Paul Martin, *Energy in Buildings and Industry*, September 2005, and *Bad Billing: the costs; Better Billing: the benefits*, Energy Watch, 2005
5   *Sustainable Energy – Response to the Government's "Energy Policy: Key Issues for Consultation"* Sustainable Development Commission, 2002
6   Energy Savings Trust report, *Schools Learning to Improve Energy Efficiency*, 2005
7   Outlined in *Guidelines to Environmental Design in Schools* DFES publication BB90, 1999
8   According to www.thinkleadership.org.uk
9   *National Best Practices Manual for Building High Performance Schools* National Clearing House for Educational Facilities, 2006
10   *Resource Management in the Education Sector* Waste Watch 2004
11   *Catering for Sustainability: the creative procurement of school meals in Italy and the UK* Kevin Morgan and Roberta Sonnino, Cardiff University, 2005
12   *The Validity of Food Miles as an Indicator of Sustainable Development* DEFRA, 2005

4 Building Your Future School

The government is making a huge investment in building and refurbishing the nation's secondary schools under the Building Schools for the Future (BSF) programme, with a smaller but still very large scheme to improve primary schools under the Primary Capital Programme. The programmes provide a one-off opportunity for school leadership teams to have a significant impact on the design of school buildings for the foreseeable future. However, there is no automatic guarantee that a new school building will be sustainable, and to achieve this requires a significant input from headteachers, governors, senior managers, teachers and local authorities. In fact, everyone in the education community has a responsibility, given the reality of climate change, to ensure that we raise the bar on implementing the principles of sustainability in any new school design or refurbishment project.

The initial waves of the BSF programme were criticised by the Chair of the Sustainable Procurement Taskforce, Sir Neville Simms, for consistently failing to meet sustainability targets. Since then the official guidance has been substantially revised and the Strategy for Change process has been re-engineered. Building plans should now meet local priorities, reduce the burden on local authorities and produce proposals that are both radical and robust. Hopefully.

CABE (the Commission for Architecture and the Built Environment) has been given a brief to ensure that sustainability is part of every design brief, but school leadership teams still need to have clear ideas about the level of sustainability they want in their design, be it a new build or a refurbishment. To help them, designs that incorporate principles of sustainability have been made available in *Exemplar Designs: concepts and ideas* DFES, 2003; *Schools for the Future: transforming schools*, DFES, 2004; *Schools for the Future: designing school grounds*, DFES, 2006: and *Schools for the Future: design of sustainable schools case studies*, DFES, 2006.

As a result of the DfES's Year of Action in 2006–7 schools are now expected to:

   significantly reduce their dependency upon fossil fuels

   increase the biodiversity of their school grounds

   reduce their demands for water and energy

   purchase in ways that follow sustainability principles

   decrease the volumes of waste produced both in construction and in day-to-day operations

   source building materials for their construction and refurbishment in as sustainable a manner as possible

   involve their communities in their future development plans.

Whilst construction industry and architectural experts are responsible for the outcomes, the visions to be created under this programme are the responsibility of school leadership teams, governors, their communities and local authorities. Success requires that all these have a clear understanding of sustainability criteria and can act as "knowledgeable clients". This may mean members of the senior leadership team committing themselves to personal professional development that focuses on sustainable development.

The practicalities of building a school are too much to add to staff or governors' existing responsibilities, and a school has to appoint a team to manage the project, with members given the necessary time to devote to it. It makes sense for at least one of the team to be seconded full time to managing the project and others allocated special time for it. Evidence from early BSF programmes indicates that up to 50 per cent of the working week of any school-based individual working on a BSF project will need to be devoted to it.

For governors the work should not be as great, but it is still likely to be a good idea to free a governor from their other responsibilities in order to concentrate on the project. It may also be necessary to enlist onto the programme someone from outside the school who can provide guidance and advice on sustainable approaches to ensure the principles are adhered to throughout the build. Funding for all of this should be included by the school in their submission about the design brief.

The members of the project team may well be stepping into the unknown and so will need access to training and ongoing advice. Professional development therefore needs to be an integral part of the basic contractual agreement. This way, what might seem at first to be a heavy burden should prove to be quite manageable. The team needs to understand:

procurement practices

design and construction practices

sustainable design approaches

regulatory frameworks for sustainability, as applied to construction.

The design of a sustainable school will require some future thinking about education as a process and the environment in which it is to be taught. The school should be able to deliver its core functions but be flexible enough in its design to accommodate future change easily. Thus the school should be designed to meet identified possible future community use, such as health services, further education and adult sports use.

It is very important that all contractors should be committed to and understand clearly the principles of sustainability, as well as providing a contractual commitment to its practice on site, and *a priori* evidence of this commitment should be made available to the leadership team of the school.

Understanding the programme

The Building Schools for the Future programme is the largest single investment made by government in improving school

Aims of Building Schools for the Future

BSF seeks to promote buildings that:

minimize adverse impacts on the environment during construction and in use, while enhancing the natural surroundings

help to encourage wider student achievement through being flexible for the future

are built cost-efficiently but sustainably

are designed to aid students' working

take fully into account their impact on the surrounding environment by seeking to maintain biodiversity within the location and by avoiding unnecessary pollution

make use of modern methods of construction wherever possible.

buildings for more than 50 years. It is not simply a building programme! The aim is to create learning environments fit for the 21st century, to enable every child and member of the learning community to have access to continuing education in a way that reflects the needs of the community. It means producing schools that are suited to meet the agendas for personalization, extended schools, Every Child Matters and workforce reform.

To deliver the BSF programme the then DfES set up a new body, Partnership for Schools (PfS). PfS manages the overall national programme and works with local authorities to plan how to use BSF funds to transform education in their areas.

Initial research findings by Partnership for Schools[1] into the initial waves of BSF programmes underline that consultation with all clients involved should be seen as a high priority before programmes are started. The research indicated that insufficient attention was being paid to the thoughts of students and the wider community in the planning for new builds. Consulting headteachers and governors was seen by local authorities as being extremely important, but was not always followed through successfully. But, and it is a large "but", consulting with students and the wider communities was seen as significantly less important.

The conclusion that could be drawn, given that the programme is meant to be about the future for students and communities, is that if local authorities do not pursue working with students and the wider community, leadership teams will have to do it instead. For these purposes the wider community of the school should include parents, local businesses and those who live in the vicinity of the proposed school. Such consultation should start before the school gets involved in planning discussions with the local authority and need to continue for far longer than is the case at present.

PfS research reinforced the findings of an Audit Commission report of 2003 on school buildings. This indicated that consortium bidders for contracts realize that not all local authorities are the same and that considerable differences in expertise exist between them. This puts yet more pressure on school leaders to be fully conversant with the processes and have clarity about the importance of sustainability. Furthermore, in 2007 the House of Commons Select Committee report into BSF found that sustainability was not included sufficiently in the early waves of the programme and asked that the recommendations of the Sustainable Procurement Task Force be implemented in future projects. The Select Committee also found that insufficient time was being given to involving a wider audience in the planning process.

So what does a member of the leadership team need to know?

The Process of BSF

Getting established

BSF, which started in 2005–6, is a rolling programme that is being developed in fifteen waves, starting at different times for different local authorities. They will not necessarily find that they receive all the BSF money at once but that it may come in two or more tranches. They are expected to look at provision across their whole area and make judgments about what is required over the pattern of schools, rather than simply look at individual schools for possible rebuild or refurbishment. They have to create a "strategic vision for the future of education" in their local area and at the same time create a strategic business case for using BSF to achieve that vision. This is called a "Strategy for Change" (see page 52), and was introduced into the fourth wave of BSF. It is the first formal component of the BSF approvals process.

Only when they have received formal DCSF approval of their Strategy for Change can local authorities submit an Outline Business Case (OBC) for BSF investment, which should contain detailed plans for the initial phase of the BSF work programme, and will be used as for a means of seeking to produce expressions of interest. This then leads to the opening of a competition for contract, whose outcome will be the identification of a preferred bidder.

At this point a Local Education Partnership (LEP) is created to manage the project. The LEP is constructed as a public-private partnership with ownership split 10 per cent local authority, 80 per cent successful bidder and 10 per cent Partnership for Schools (PfS). It is charged with ensuring that all aspects of the planned programme are delivered. As the strategic commissioner the LEP has a long-term partnering agreement with the local authority and separate contracts with it for individual school projects. These individual contracts can either be PFI or Capital/Design Build.

The business of the LEP is to:

> provide/procure the "Partnering Services" as set out in the Strategic Partnering Agreement (the BSF standard partner agreement form between the LA and the LEP, which will in turn will be based on the strategic business case of each local authority)

> provide additional services as envisaged under the Strategic Partnering Agreement

> work with the supply chain to achieve partnering consistent with that envisaged under the Strategic Partnering Agreement.

During the initial development phase for the standard LEP there should be a business cycle of 18 months comprised of four distinct stages:

post-financial-close of a project when work has not started on new development work (6 months)

development work on the next stage to Stage 1 Approval (3 months)

development work on the next stage to Stage 2 Approval (6 months)

financial close of the development stage (3 months).

These will be undertaken in accordance with the LEP's business plan, which will also cover income, costs and capital requirements for the LEP as well as setting out corporate business objectives and targets.

The delivery process

There are distinctive elements to the BSF delivery process.

1. Project initiation

Initial discussions produce a project initiation document. This is the base document against which the project manager and project board can assess progress. The LA identifies the case for the process and identifies the schools to be involved. The relevant schools should then be consulted from this stage on and should therefore have a team in place to promote their thoughts about the school development. This is the time to emphasize that sustainability should be an overarching framework for the programme.

2. Setting the vision and the strategic business case

The leadership team is required to examine every aspect of what is taught, how it is taught and how their schools are to be managed. The vision must encompass innovation and enable teaching and learning to be positively transformed. The Sustainable Development Commission report *Every Child's Future Matters* (2007), for example, suggests that the ECM agenda could be delivered through a sustainable focus that recognizes the Sustainable Schools and ECM agendas as mutually supportive. This is the point at which to consult children about the vision for their schools. As we have seen, research makes clear that members of any leadership team involved in a BSF programme *must insist* on an extended consultation period being at the heart of the programme.

The outcome of this stage of the process is the Strategy for Change, which should tie together the authority's strategies for local education and for its whole school estate – thus encouraging it to focus simultaneously on the two principal elements of the BSF programme. This Strategy for Change has two parts. Part 1 is the Key Challenges and Objectives. It is the "what is to be done" component and should specify how the local BSF proposals will address both the remit and locally agreed priorities. Among a large list of requirements it should show:

how every school in the programme will change after BSF investment

current achievement data

what extended services the school will offer

the school's present and future governance arrangements

the social and economic profile of the community served by the school.

It should also clearly state the key performance indicators such as Every Child Matters agenda, diversity and choice, and identify existing and planned consultations about the programme.

Part 2 is the Detail and Delivery section. This shows how the authority intends to achieve its objectives. It is the "how it will be done" component. The challenges faced by the local authority in terms of educational outcomes, diversity, choice and fair access should be identified and how the BSF programme will help it address these issues.

This section also identifies how the authority will seek to meet the requirements of the community, which may include plans for re-organization of provision, including the development of academies and trust schools, provision for gifted and talented pupils, and innovative use of ICT as well as the ECM and SEN agendas. The document should identify how schools are to be assisted with advice and how proposals will be consulted on with other local stakeholders. There must be a proposal for a formal consultation process. The proposals should also address key estate priorities and project planning.

At this point it is vital for schools to identify their requirements for sustainability, such as:

the sustainable procurement of materials

the development of a principle of zero waste from site

an ICT procurement process which seeks to minimize energy consumption and follows principles of sustainability

the importance of sustainable procurement practices being implemented by all contractors.

The LA must consult widely on its proposals at this stage, which gives schools, students and the community another and crucially important opportunity to stress the need for sustainability in the finished buildings. This is particularly important if the local authority does not itself have a clear commitment to sustainability.

There may be resistance to focusing on sustainability among local authority officers. This may be expressed on the grounds of cost. Such views need to be challenged. You may need to remind them of government targets for sustainability in schools and point out that it is much more expensive to fit sustainable capacity into a finished building than to incorporate it from the outset.

There is plenty of international research evidence that makes it clear that building schools sustainably need not cost more, if a whole-life cost analysis is undertaken. The earlier sustainable features are built into the design the lower the cost.[2] In fact, 80 per cent of a building's costs are in the operation and maintenance programmes pursued over its lifetime, so if sustainable specifications are applied up front the total operating and maintenance costs of a building will be much cheaper, as well as impacting significantly less on the climate.

The early BSF projects can teach useful lessons, both in terms of the building design itself and in the processes used to realize it.

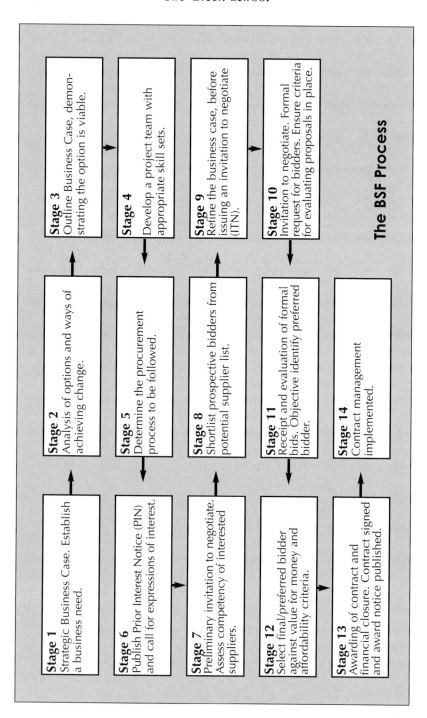

The BSF Process

Stage 1
Strategic Business Case. Establish a business need.

Stage 2
Analysis of options and ways of achieving change.

Stage 3
Outline Business Case, demonstrating the option is viable.

Stage 4
Develop a project team with appropriate skill sets.

Stage 5
Determine the procurement process to be followed.

Stage 6
Publish Prior Interest Notice (PIN) and call for expressions of interest.

Stage 7
Preliminary invitation to negotiate. Assess competency of interested suppliers.

Stage 8
Shortlist prospective bidders from potential supplier list.

Stage 9
Refine the business case, before issuing an invitation to negotiate (ITN).

Stage 10
Invitation to negotiate. Formal request for bidders. Ensure criteria for evaluating proposals in place.

Stage 11
Receipt and evaluation of formal bids. Objective identify preferred bidder.

Stage 12
Select final/preferred bidder against value for money and affordability criteria.

Stage 13
Awarding of contract and financial closure. Contract signed and award notice published.

Stage 14
Contract management implemented.

The local authority's plans should reflect the lessons from these, specifically:

> that opportunities for smaller construction companies and local sustainable supply chains have been identified and included in the processes;

> that proposals minimize the consumption of non-renewable resources, and minimize the use of energy by re-using recycled materials and reducing pollution;

> that the cost estimates are as accurate as possible and have been tested;

> that opportunities for co-occupation of community facilities are included in the design programme, with a wide strategic focus;

> that post-occupancy evaluation is included in all proposals that should be shared with PfS and the DCSF.

(Stages 1 and 2 of "The BSF Process" diagram)

3. Business case development

After the strategic case has been outlined the local authority details the scope, affordability, risks, procurement route and timetable of the project. The project is detailed and costed and submitted to the DCSF and PfS for approval. Once approved, the authority can begin procuring a partner to deliver on its programme.

It is important that sustainability is included as a core factor in the programme before submission to the DCSF and PfS, as any subsequent change would have to be submitted as a variation to the programme and is unlikely to be approved. *(Stages 3 and 4)*

4. Procurement planning

Documentation is prepared in order to publish a "notice" or advertisement for the contract tender process. There are a set of standard documents for this process. This material must be closely read by the leadership team. *(Stages 5 and 6)*

5. Procurement

Following the publication of the contract the local authority receives and evaluates expressions of interest. A longlist of bidders is drawn up and they are then invited to submit outline solutions. Based on this longlist, a shortlist of usually three bidders is produced, who are requested to draw up detailed solutions. Out of this a preferred bidder is identified, with whom the LA and PfS will form the Local Education Partnership. The Final Business Case is then submitted to PfS and DCSF for approval, outlining the proposed contractual arrangements, including any variations from the outline business case. *(Stages 7 to 12)*

6. Contractual close

Once approval is given by DCSF and PfS for funding, the local authority and PfS contract with the preferred supplier. At this point construction can begin. *(Stage 13)*

7. Construction stage

As the initial BSF process involved groups of schools and their leadership teams across a local authority, the local authority is expected to develop a team approach across all schools affected by it. However each individual school should establish an in-house team which should work to represent the interests of their own school from stage 1.

The local authority is responsible for agreeing a total funding envelope for the project and the allocation of funds to each school build through the Strategy for Change process. Schools which have been built in the last 15 years will not be included in the resource allocation, unless they are being enlarged to accommodate an increase in pupil numbers.

Once the scope and procurement route for each individual project has been established the school will be expected to develop a working group of governors and staff to contribute to the design brief and to evaluate all proposals. At this point the team should research and consult widely with students, parents and the community at large, and investigate the support offered through the Commission for Architecture and the Built Environment (CABE), the Sorrell Foundation, the Royal Institute of British Architects (RIBA) and the local authority to ensure that a truly sustainable design is produced.

The LEP procures the delivery of the project to ensure that timescales are adhered to and costs are controlled.

It does this by setting up Special Purposes Vehicles (SPVs). An SPV is a consortium of companies (for example, in construction, ICT, finance and facilities management) established to deliver a specific project within the BSF programme.

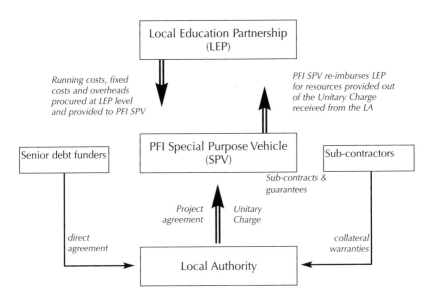

The LEP and the PFI Special Purpose Vehicle (SPV)
(adapted from PFS, *BSF Economic Guidance Note: economics of the LEP*, 2007)

The supply-chain process of the programme is expected to be monitored and tested regularly for best value. A critical factor in determining the success of the BSF programme will be the extent to which the LEP can develop effective partnerships with those in the supply chain. It's important to identify that "best value" does not mean cheapest, and that life-cycle analysis is undertaken to assess the value for money expected of the materials used in construction. If sustainability has been built into the specifications, then this should not be a difficulty. *(Stage 14)*

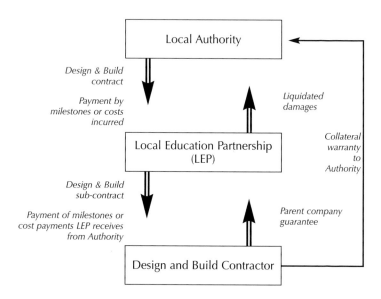

Flow of funds between the local authority and the contractor
(adapted from PFS, *BSF Economic Guidance Note: economics of the LEP*, 2007)

8. Post-occupancy evaluation

The finished building should be assessed against the plans after the school has moved in, provided this has been included in the earliest stages of the specification. The objective is to gauge satisfaction with the buildings and services, and feed useful information into later stages of the national BSF programme.

Getting the design right

If you are a governor you need to ask yourself the question, "What should I expect from a sustainable school design?" In essence, it should be about applied good sense! It should be about building something to the highest quality standard with maximum environmental and social benefit, with a focus on whole life-cycle cost analysis.

The functional requirements, both for now and the future, include the impacts on the building's users, the amount and kinds of resources consumed in construction and operation, pollution levels, waste outputs, the impact on the health of users and the biodiversity of the community in which it sits. This means they should be:

efficient in their use of resources in their construction

efficient to operate

minimize their impact on the environment with reduced CO_2 emissions, minimized energy and water consumption and significantly reduced waste outputs

fit for purpose and flexible in their operation so as to meet the needs of the community they serve.

What should you be looking for in a sustainable school design?

Ideally, a sustainable school should provide comfortable conditions for all who work in it. It should provide a healthy environment, with excellent lighting and fresh air without relying on mechanical systems. At the same time the building should provide a resource for enquiry into sustainability and be an exemplar to the wider community of the need for sustainable approaches.

Ventilation

The ideal is a naturally ventilated building, with appropriate window design. Maintaining a high level of indoor air quality impacts positively on student performance and absenteeism.

Natural lighting

Lighting predominantly by daylight should be a priority. With sufficient commitment from the outset it is possible to design a building that uses daylight, while avoiding summer overheating and managing solar gain only in winter. This starts with a proper orientation of the building (see next page). The architects should be asked to look at external shading, high levels of insulation, high-level glazing specifications, clerestory windows, light tubes and light shelves.

Fabric of the building

The material fabric of the building can also cause significant design issues. In particular the use of heavy or light building materials needs to be evaluated on a case-by-case basis. Heavyweight materials, such as concrete brick or block, absorb heat during the day and reduce the immediate impact of heat gains from people, equipment and the sun. However, such "gains" need to be disposed of overnight by naturally ventilating the building, which may produce security issues. Lightweight building materials, such as glulam (glued laminated timber), timber framing, bamboo, straw and aerated concrete block, respond quickly to internal and solar gain, which can lead to short-term overheating. Natural low-toxicity materials such as natural wood, cellulose insulation materials and low-odour paints promote a healthy internal environment. Avoidance of plastic-based finishes allows the building to "breathe", reducing the risk of surface condensation and mould growth.

It is also important to identify the use of recycled and environmentally sound materials in the design process specifications. You could identify as one of your priorities that a good percentage of materials to be used in the construction should be from recycled materials or sourced from sustainable sources. It is quite possible to do this: the Waste Resources Action programme has undertaken studies into use of materials in schools and found that there is significant scope for recycled materials to be used in the BSF programme.[3] There is a double gain to be made: the combined force of schools looking for such materials provides the impetus for greater marketing of products, while there is less CO_2 output in their production.

The design brief for St Francis of Assisi School in Kensington, Liverpool stressed the need for a building that would facilitate environmental education, model good environmental practice and offer itself as an educational resource. The building is concrete-framed and was constructed by a flat-slab method with floor slabs, while its basement walls have been left exposed for thermal reasons. The external walls are clad in Douglas fir. Sandstone excavated from the site provides the topping for the brown roofs, which are planted with sedum. Internal finishes have been designed to minimize environmental impact.

Orientation

The orientation of the building can contribute significantly to whether a school achieves or fails to achieve true sustainability standards. *Building on an east-west axis gives classrooms a more diffuse light suitable for day lighting.* Glare can be controlled and heat gain reduced. On the other hand, a long north-south axis exposes windows to low-angle sun with more glare and heat gain.

The location of classrooms that will use a lot of equipment, such those for ICT or food technology, away from areas of solar gain may make it possible to ventilate them naturally.

Health

The term "sick building syndrome" came into use in the 1970s to describe how some people felt ill in buildings put up over the previous decade. Poor ventilation, combined with chemical contamination from indoor surfaces such as carpets, paint finishes, manufactured wood products and moulds, gave some users headaches, nausea and feelings of listlessness. In contrast, using natural materials and low-odour paint finishes, and avoiding plastics-based finishes, will help promote healthy indoor environments.

Occupancy levels

Sustainable buildings that do not rely on mechanical systems for ventilation are more sensitive to overcrowding than ones that are air-conditioned. Therefore, it is important to consider the occupancy levels of a building before decisions regarding room size/capacity are reached. This requires some careful forward thinking and will take time, taking into consideration whole-life costing.

Energy systems

Energy systems in sustainably designed schools should be affordable to install and run and simple to manage and maintain. As a first stage seek to minimise, where economically possible, the total energy demand of the building. But even a low-energy system does not guarantee against waste. An energy management system should be included that monitors and identifies usage throughout the school. That said, a system is only as good as the people who manage it so it is likely that you will have to cost for training for those responsible.

Aim to include sustainable technologies in the system chosen: solar thermal water heating, ground-source heat pumps, photo-voltaic power, wind generation, biomass and other renewable energy technologies. They will not only contribute to the building's sustainability but also to the curriculum by illustrating to the students these technologies in practice.

Cost is often identified as a reason for not implementing sustainable energy technologies, but once again a whole-life analysis needs to be undertaken. ("A one-time investment premium of less than 1 per cent of first costs can increase energy efficiency over standard building code practices by 20–30 per cent," New York State Energy Research and Development Authority, 2008.)

In any event, only devices with an A energy rating should be included. Ensure all air supply and extraction systems have heat recovery processes.

School grounds

The school site is a potential source of biodiversity and hence a teaching tool that could not be closer to hand. The government manifesto *Learning Outside the Classroom*[4] states that every student should experience the world outside the classroom as an essential part of learning and personal development. Moreover, the learning experience outside the classroom enhances learning inside the classroom, by providing a context for it. Learners can engage with the world as they experience it. Helping people to learn in this way is a powerful driver towards improved student performance. Learning outside the classroom is also seen as making a significant contribution to delivery of the Every Child Matters agenda.

School grounds potentially provide a learning resource for both formal and informal learning, and give students the chance to explore sustainability as part of their school curriculum (see chapter 7). The charity devoted to getting children to learning and playing in school grounds, Learning through Landscapes, has published a pack with which to undertake an evaluation of the school grounds as a learning experience for students.[5]

Water usage

As we have seen, schools that use water efficiently reduce their operating costs through lower meter and lower sewerage charges. An appreciable saving can be made by collecting non-drinking ("grey") water for use in toilets and landscape irrigation, as, for example, has been shown by St Francis of Assisi School in Liverpool. Chesswood Middle School in Worthing fitted a range of water-saving equipment, including urinal controls and self-closing push taps, and as a result the school's water consumption dropped by 73 per cent and they saved £3000 on their annual water bill.

Waste management and recycling

Establishing the principle of minimal waste at the beginning of construction will ensure that significant questions are raised about the supply chain. Encourage the builders to source materials that have a low environmental impact throughout their lives. This principle does not apply just to the fabric of a school, but also to the equipment bought to put in it. Tackling this calls for setting a policy that the lifespan of products will be taken into account when considering which ones to buy, and requiring those responsible for purchases to consider sustainability. Many products like printers and computers have extended life cycles and recyclability built into their manufacture.

Facilities and processes can be designed into any new-build school to encourage recycling of all materials. To that end every classroom could be designed and equipped to encourage point-of-source separation of waste materials. Each classroom should have clearly identified receptacles for different materials so that pupils can be taught the importance and value of separated recycling. Ensure that recycling facilities are provided on the school site and that contracts are made with appropriate waste management organisations.

Transport

Providing the facilities and security for cycle use by students is a high priority, and funds for this are available through Sustrans, while school travel grants are available from the travel advisers at the local authority on completion of a school travel plan.

A new build gives you the chance to consider travel from the roots up. As well as cycling, how about (in primary schools) a "walking bus" scheme in which parents help in escorting pupils to school in groups? Restrict car parking on the school site and encourage car sharing among staff. Make sure the design separates different types of transport to eliminate any risk to pedestrians or cyclists. Footpaths and cycle paths should be designed to avoid crossing access routes and car parks, while separate cycle access points should be considered a priority. Think also of drop-off points. You could create a policy that says only parents who travel more than a certain distance should use them.

Finally, involve the local authority's Safer Routes to School team and its travel advisers.

BREEAM

"BREEAM Schools" stands for the Building Research Establishment Environmental Assessment Method for Schools, a tool that has been developed by the Building Research Establishment for environmental assessment of new school builds. Its application is designed to set environmental targets for the building of schools, and it is a requirement of capital funding for new and refurbishment projects that they achieve no less than a very good rating under the BREEAM standard. Buildings are assessed externally and awarded credits according to the level of performance in nine environmental categories. These are:

management

energy use

health and well-being

pollution

transport

land use

ecology

materials

water.

However, as an enquiry by the House of Commons Education and Skills Committee made clear in a report in 2007 a BREEAM score of "very good" does not in fact make the school truly sustainable. In addition, the Sustainable Development Commission said that BREEAM "does not encapsulate a vision for sustainable school buildings and is therefore unable to inspire, and is not designed to assist with the basic design decisions necessary to make the most of the current capital investment decisions"(2007). While the method is a reasonable tool for guiding teams in improving the sustainability credentials of a building, meeting the BREEAM standard does not go far enough towards identifying ways of reducing the carbon emissions that are required by government.

References

1   *Project Planning Guidance (including Project Initiation Document)* www.p4s.org.uk/documents, October 2007
2   *The Cost and Benefits of Green Buildings: a report to California's Sustainable Building Task Force* J. Kats, L.Alevantis, A.Bierman, E.Mills, J.Perlman, Sustainable Building Task Force, Sacramento, California, 2003; *Introduction to Sustainable Design* Jog Jin Kim, University of Michigan, 1998; *Developing Life Cycle Assessment Tools for Buildings in Hong Kong* Raymond Yau, ARUP 2004; *Assessing Secondary School Design Quality* CABE, 2006
3   *Higher Recycled Content and Waste Minimization in Schools Procurement* Davis Langdon, 2004
4   *Learning Outside the Classroom* DCSF, 2007
5   *Workout: a toolkit aimed at all those involved with improving the use, design and management of secondary school grounds* Learning through Landscapes, 2005

5 Making Sustainability Core

"Education for sustainable development enables people to develop the knowledge, values and skills to participate in decisions about the way we do things individually and collectively, both locally and globally, that will improve the quality of life now, without damaging the planet for the future." *The National Curriculum*[1]

Schools that want to make real progress in delivering the message about sustainability need to ensure that sustainable development is one of the central tenets that they exemplify. If you are going to take sustainability seriously it means it has to be a driver for everything that you do as an organization. There is no simple way to do this, since while there are many exemplars, each school is unique. To start means asking yourselves some searching questions.

Are sustainable development principles clearly identified as a primary driver to the functioning of this school?
It is unlikely that schools will become successful at delivering the sustainable development agenda without the enthusiasm and support of headteachers, senior managers and governors.

Is there a real desire among the leadership team to address sustainability issues?
Behaviour change needs to occur at a collective, social level if it is to occur at all! Thus leadership teams need to develop among themselves and in their staff a collective desire for it.

Human beings are social creatures and learn by example. We model our behaviour on those we see around us, especially those who are held in regard. Therefore schools, as dominant institutions in their communities, have an extremely influential role in modelling environmentally sustainable behaviour for their pupils and the wider community to emulate.

For leadership teams in schools, losing some existing attitudes may be necessary if they are to commit the school to sustainability. This is best done in a supportive social environment.

How important is care to our thinking and planning?

A belief in the importance of care for the environment is central to delivering education for sustainable development (ESD). However, the environment is not the only concern. The principle of care is at the heart of ESD – care for those in the school and for the community as well as for the environment. This means nurturing a caring approach towards the members of the school community and the external community it serves, as well as developing a responsibility for future generations who may inhabit its community.

Where does sustainability feature in our policies?

Your school should make a clear statement that sustainability is a core goal in the school and is identified clearly in all relevant school policy documents (i.e. asset management, lettings, curriculum, health and safety, nutritional standards and school session times). The school asset management plan should include a clear statement of a plan to improve environmental practice, and this aim should be apparent at the heart of the school improvement/development plan.

How are our structures and processes addressing sustainability?

This will appear in clearly identified objectives, appropriate targets and timescales, and monitoring and evaluation systems.

How is our school involving stakeholders in this process?

The school should identify how it will involve all stakeholders in the decision-making processes it undertakes. The sustainable school sees all of them as central to its functioning and ensures that every effort is made to involve them through regular consultations with local communities on how the school might meet their needs, by working with the student body on issues of design for sustainability and by providing access to design professionals for local groups to facilitate their thinking.

How does our curriculum address sustainable development?
The school curriculum should clearly address the statutory requirement to teach about sustainable development but should also include opportunities to develop in pupils a commitment to life-long learning about sustainability. For more on the curriculum, see chapter 7.

Does the school curriculum promote a global outlook?
Global citizenship already features in the English school curriculum, and one of government's aims is that each school will have an established International School Partner by 2010. Pupils need to understand how their future is inextricably linked to and affected by the lives and decisions of others across the world.

The way the curriculum is delivered should identify the links between society, the environment and the economy. It needs to make explicit the needs and the rights of present and future generations and the relationship between human rights and access to resources and power. Are the local and global implications of our actions as individuals and as societies identified? Are the kinds of actions individuals can take in response to local and global issues clearly addressed?

Is the approach to sustainability in the curriculum integrated?
ESD can be regarded as many things – as environmental science and management, as values and behavioural change, and as social criticism.

The focus within the curriculum should be on developing a critical and analytical approach among pupils. As any teacher knows, just preaching a message will be counter-productive. It is through dialogue that pupils can decide what is technically possible, culturally appropriate and morally and politically correct. To achieve a cohesive approach may well require professional development for teachers. The Qualifications and Curriculum Authority (QCA) is already examining this for the training of the next generation of teachers, but in the meantime it is provided by non-governmental and charitable organizations such as WWF, Heads Teachers and Industry (HTI), Teachers in Development Education (TIDE) and Eco-Schools.

Of course, busy teachers may feel that they are coping with enough changes without learning how to deliver ESD. But for those not attracted by the carrot of believing that ESD is highly worthwhile, there will almost certainly eventually be sticks from central government. Ofsted and the DCSF have made it clear that government is thoroughly committed to delivering on sustainability and that schools are an integral part of the mechanism.

The present subject-based secondary curriculum could deliver the ESD framework but the approach needs to be carefully thought through. Some pioneering schools have already shown that ESD can be delivered at the same time as significantly improving pupil performance (see chapter 6).

How does our approach to the Every Child Matters agenda fit in with a sustainable development framework?
The DCSF has also made it clear that it believes that sustainable schools are guided by "a commitment to caring for oneself, for others across cultures, distances and generations and with a commitment to caring for the environment" (2007). Thus sustainable schools have a focus on developing a positive attitude towards social responsibility in their pupils. Sustainability is an aspect of the ECM agenda, not apart from it.

ECM recognizes that growing up is a process of understanding yourself and your place in the world. Three specific goals are being healthy, making a positive contribution to society and achieving economic well-being, which chime perfectly with ESD. And the Sustainable Development Commission has identified in *Every Child's Future Matters* (2007) that the outcomes of the

ECM agenda can be achieved through a focus on local and global environments.

What steps is our school taking to undertake a different approach to purchasing?
As we have seen, this entails identifying the whole-life costs of goods or services when making spending decisions, and ensuring that analysing whole-life costs is identified in a procurement policy as a prerequisite for any purchases. This policy message should be clearly communicated to all staff and developed as a series of protocols.

Are strategies for reduction, re-use and recycling embedded in our school?
The best way of teaching is by example. So visibly tackling waste in schools is of double benefit. This means not just leaving it to individuals but having school policies that address the three key waste issues:

throwaway products

excessive packaging

buying degradable or dating materials in quantities larger than required at the time.

The last one does not mean choosing to ignore the benefits of bulk purchasing but realizing that, if not stored and handled properly, materials can degrade or become out of date, and ultimately be disposed of as waste. A careful analysis of the nature of the materials to be purchased is needed before buying in bulk to store some for future use.

Do we do what we can to reduce waste?
The first step in managing waste in schools is to analyse what is being produced. "If you can't measure it you can't manage it" may be an old mantra but it is certainly true in this case. This means developing and regularly conducting waste audits.

Pupils can usefully undertake some of the work as a curriculum exercise (obviously excluding any materials that might be hazardous). The audit should identify:

how much waste is produced by the school

where it is generated

what kinds of materials go to waste

the costs associated with collection and disposal

Reducing waste paper

The paper and cardboard-based waste that makes up the majority of waste produced by schools in the UK can be reduced in a number of ways:

ensuring that all printers and photocopiers in the school are set to default to two-sided printing mode

subjecting all purchasing decisions made by the school to a recyclability analysis before purchase: if it can't be recycled should it be purchased?

buying easily refillable consumables for printers and similar items

composting relevant wastes, such as fruit

encouraging pupils to use refillable bottles and to reduce the amount of packaging they bring into school with their packed lunches – having special no-waste days may help

encouraging all contracted suppliers to take back packaging as part of their contractual obligations

finding extra bins for classrooms and corridors, and space for them, to encourage source separation of waste materials

reducing what the school is spending through careful analysis of consumption patterns throughout the year

re-using business items such as envelopes

encouraging staff to save documents electronically wherever possible, in order to reduce printing and to increase the sharing of curriculum material

distributing the parents' newsletter electronically where possible

ensuring compliance with the WEEE (Waste Electronic and Electrical Equipment) Directive.

what is or is not happening in the school to reduce the volumes of waste

who, if anyone, has responsibility for the management of this waste.

You may find that your school produces significant quantities of waste materials that are classified as "hazardous", such as fluorescent tubes, redundant computer equipment, televisions and spent batteries. The law on disposal of hazardous waste[2] stipulates that these have to be separated from the general waste stream of the school and disposed of properly. Before disposal they must be stored securely, and after disposal there should be evidence that they have been disposed of safely.

Schools that produce more than 200 kilos of such waste a year (which might mean as few as 10 computer monitors) may need to be registered with the Environment Agency.

Do we manage energy as part of school development/ improvement planning?
The 10 per cent most energy-inefficient schools use more than twice the energy of the most efficient schools.

Research in 2007 into carbon footprinting in primary schools undertaken by the Building Services Research and Information Association found that there is no simple relationship between the age of its buildings and a school's energy performance and carbon output. A comparison between a Victorian school, a 1960s school and a 21st-century school concluded that the performance of the 1960s school was far worse than that of the Victorian and modern ones. And the difference in carbon footprint between the Victorian school and the 21st-century school was relatively insignificant.

This outcome indicates that the wholesale replacement of Victorian buildings by modern buildings may not automatically improve schools' carbon footprint! However, unless such buildings are sympathetically redeveloped many of their performance capabilities may be negated. Many such schools, for example, use air conditioning, which could be unnecessary if they

Refurbishing primary schools

The Primary Capital Programme calls for creative thinking and considering a variety of options. For example, it may be that recommissioning heating systems will achieve the desired energy savings without replacing older boilers, but when replacement is necessary, condensing boilers should be a priority, or, if the school has significant areas with different heating or hot water requirements, installing a decentralized boiler system might be the best answer.

When staff make purchasing decisions they should be aware that solar thermal heating for water is generally a cost-effective solution. This is not currently true of solar photovoltaic cells, but this may change and they are relatively easy to install. Generation by wind power might be a viable option for some schools (see Cassop Primary School in chapter 6), but a feasibility study is necessary first. Biomass boilers are really only realistic for new-build projects or when the school needs to convert or update existing plant from a solid fuel system. Government grants are available for all these.

For an example of a school which has led the way, see the case study of Seaton Primary School in chapter 6.

were redesigned in an energy-efficient way. A once-in-a-lifetime opportunity is provided for primary schools by the Primary Capital Programme, which envisages refurbishing rather than rebuilding the majority of primary schools in the country.

Do we use natural light as much as possible?

Daylight can give enough light in most school spaces, but it does require management. The light should be balanced, diffuse and glare-free, come from at least two directions, and be sufficient for the tasks to be performed. Too much light can be as big a problem as too little, so you may need operable shading. Exterior shading should be available to reduce solar heat gain.

However, your school will still need electric lighting. The most efficient types of bulb are fluorescent – T8 or T5. The numerical definition refers to the diameter of the tubes (in eighths of an inch) – the narrower the profile the better the optical control and efficiency. T5s and T8s can provide around 50 per cent more lighting intensity than older tubes and can be delivered with a standard or high-output design. They are best employed in any new build and refurbishment projects but should also be included as part of any rolling refurbishment of school premises.

Does our school take a flexible approach to the development of ICT?

Ever-increasing amounts are being spent by schools on the infrastructure and knowledge needed for pupils to acquire the skills and capabilities that they will require in the outside world. However, according to Professor Stephen Heppell, founder of Ultralab, the development of ICT is an organic process which changes extremely rapidly, with the result that seeking to establish standards in educational ICT is doomed to failure.[3] He argues that schools need an "agile strategy", one that constantly tests their creativity in relation to the use of ICT. Seeking to lay down standards of acceptable use, such as email policies or limiting the use of social networking sites, is an irrelevance. Schools, that is the pupils and teachers, should be about "inventing" different uses for technology. Indeed, they should be contributing seriously to questions such as whether the investment that their school is making is taking it in the right direction.

The pace of change in ICT is not about to diminish, so any planning should be in the light of understanding the rapidity of this change. For a start, schools need to conduct an audit of their present infrastructure and equipment, as well as identifying the training needs of staff, and evaluating their current procurement practices. The BECTA Total Cost of Ownership research programme points out that the average purchase cost of ICT amounts to only 25 per cent of the total cost of lifetime use. As we have said previously, buying large numbers of energy-hungry machines can have significant energy and cost implications, including air conditioning to keep them cool. When the siting of ICT is being planned, take energy consumption and heat output into consideration. It is also clear that with the rate of change in technology machines can become obsolete very quickly, with resulting high disposal costs.

Does our school operate within healthy school parameters and address the Healthy Schools agenda?

The National Healthy Schools programme builds on what schools are already doing to promote physical activity, healthy eating, and emotional well-being. It has four themes:

Personal, Social and Health Education (PSHE), including sex and relationship education (SRE) and drugs education

Healthy Eating

Physical Activity

Emotional Health and Wellbeing, including tackling bullying.

Evidence shows that there is a significant link between health improvement and educational attainment.[4]

ESD contributes to promoting the healthy schools agenda by providing opportunities for physical activity, including growing vegetables on site as part of the curriculum, and by developing school grounds so as to encourage active play. Pupil health and well-being can be compromised by exposure to pollution, excessive traffic, a lack of green space and play areas, low levels of activity and poor diets. Sustainable schools place a high value on the well-being of their pupils and the school environment.

Is the school estate used as a learning resource for the curriculum and also for the wider school community?

The government committed itself to increasing the use of school grounds in its 2007 manifesto *Learning Outside the Classroom*, which aims to raise pupil achievement through an organized, strategic approach to learning in which direct experience is of prime importance.

The Five Outcomes of Every Child Matters can be supported through a sustainable approach to developing and managing grounds. As we saw in chapter 4, school grounds can enrich teaching and learning across the whole school curriculum. They can also be used as one of your supplies of healthy food! In addition, the grounds can foster the informal curriculum by providing opportunities for contact between pupils. This is especially positive if they have been involved in helping plan the

Grounds for engaging pupils

A research paper by the Education Development Center and the Boston Schoolyard Funders Collaborative in the USA in 2000 investigated how effective school grounds are in enhancing pupil learning. It discovered that pupils were enthusiastic about the activities they were able to do in school grounds, especially hands-on enquiry-based tasks. It established that outdoor activities seemed to have a positive impact on teaching and learning. While it made clear that there was no unequivocal proof that developing school grounds guarantees improved pupil performance, it did discover that teachers find it successful, attributing this to pupils gaining hands-on experience, taking a pride of ownership in such projects, enjoying opportunities to learn kinesthetically and being offered a broader approach to the curriculum.

development of the grounds. After all, they may best know how they can use them. Moreover, involving pupils in grounds management fosters a feeling of inclusion and creates a sense of ownership.

School grounds are also a community resource, and they may be the only patch of green in a built-up environment. Members of the community could benefit from access to a well-designed school site, especially if they also have been involved in their design and development. Extended services should include the use of school facilities by the community; this might be developed by forming partnerships with other agencies and organizations.

Is the biodiversity of the site enhanced by effective management and a commitment to further develop the process on site?
Many school grounds are refuges for wildlife and are often undisturbed for many hours in the year. It is not enough to rely upon one specific member of the teaching staff to take on responsibility for them, because if they leave or find themselves with increasing responsibilities then the grounds are often neglected.

As part of a positive approach to the encouragement of wildlife, parts of the school grounds could be designated as wildlife areas

The side effects of site enhancement: case study

Royton and Crompton School in Manchester used landfill tax grant to improve recreation and learning facilities on their school site. It did this by creating a patchwork of habitats.

Site enhancement was carried out over several years and across year groups. The primary objectives were to:

- improve opportunities for physical and social recreation for the school and the local community

- develop a nature and activity area

- involve pupils in the design and realization of the project

- show pupils how they could make a difference by improving their own environment

- enhance their links with the local community.

Staff and pupils worked with a local environment group and Groundwork to plant trees and wild flowers. These included beech hedges which pupils had collected from saplings at a local nature reserve, wild flowers bought with money raised by recycling at the school, and trees donated by local organizations. The process involved the pupils learning about sustainable development in a practical way as well as promoting their understanding of citizenship.

The senior leadership team at the school found that pupils showed increased understanding of environmental issues as well as increased motivation, while at the same time the biodiversity of the school grounds was much increased. In addition, giving the community access reduced the incidence of anti-social behaviour.

and left "wild". While they may not look as "cared for" as might be expected of a school, green deserts and amenity flower beds are less likely to attract wildlife.

Existing grounds can be enhanced through positive management and additional planting, while new ones can be constructed according to local biodiversity plans, which can be accessed on the UK Biodiversity Action Plan website at www.ukbap.org.uk. There are several organizations that are happy to work with schools on their grounds, first being the local authority, but also charities such as the BTCV, Groundwork UK, Learning through Landscapes, the Wildlife Trusts, the RSPB and the Woodland Trust. They can help develop the school grounds to create meadows, ponds, log piles, bird boxes, hedges and trees that provide shelter for animals and birds, as well as creating vegetable, herb and flower gardens.

Does the school promote carbon-neutral travel to and from the site, by encouraging cycling and walking and through campaigns to reduce volumes of vehicular traffic on site?
In 2003 the government published an action plan *Travelling to School*[5] designed to stimulate strategic approaches to school travel. Its aims are to promote walking, cycling and public transport and to reduce car dependency for journeys to and from school.

School and regional travel advisers, of whom there are some 250 in England, including one in each local authority, will help schools develop and implement action plans, and provide information on what else is being done in the area.

Where pupils live too far from their schools to cycle or walk you could discuss providing a bus service with the local authority and local transport operators, or increase the availability and attractiveness of existing ones. And where private motor transport remains the only option for some pupils, why not encourage parents to share cars?

How does our school promote the principles of sustainability to our wider community and how is it evaluating that influence?
A committed school will realize that educating people about sustainability does not stop at the school gates. To engage with the local community needs a communications strategy that actively promotes ESD.

But not all communication is good communication. People screen out messages that are not well targeted. Providing information is not enough: on its own it can raise awareness but probably not lead to attitude or behaviour change, while exhortation generally fails to work. The answer for schools is to be living exemplars of the sustainable development approaches they seek to promote, and then to define the message you want to give your community. It needs to be an inspiring and above all a practical one, and to show that people can make a difference.

Here are a few ideas:

Get as many people as possible in the local community to pledge a personal commitment to behaviour change.

Give publicity to even small changes that individuals make in their behaviour.

Make a large visible commitment at the school, such as fitting a highly visible wind turbine.

Identify community champions for sustainability.

Hold specific climate change events for the community.

Moving forward

The questions identified in this chapter are a starting point! They will help to move the school's thinking forward, but a starting point is all they are. Achieving sustainability in our schools will take time and a fair degree of intellectual challenge, but it will be worthwhile in the end.

"Sustainable development ... promotes good governance, healthy living, innovation, life–long learning and all forms of economic growths, which secure the natural capital upon which we depend. It reinforces social harmony and seeks to secure each individual's prospects of leading a fulfilling life." (Jonathon Porritt, 2004[6])

References

1   The English National Curriculum, QCA, 1999
2   The Hazardous Waste (England and Wales) Regulations 2005
3   See http://www.heppell.net/weblog/stephen/
4   See research from NFER and Thomas Coram Institute, 2004
5   DfES/0520/2003
6   Jonathan Porritt, "Sustainable Development Past and Present", Patrick Geddes Lecture, 23 November 2004, Sustainable Development Commission, http://www.sd-commission.org.uk/publications/.

6 Best Practice in Sustainability

It can be hard to be out there on your own developing a sustainable school. There's no legal requirement to be sustainable at present, and the DCSF and Ofsted, although extremely keen to see the development of sustainable schools, won't (as yet!) penalise you if you take no steps towards sustainability. So where is the incentive?

In reality it all comes down to your desire to effect significant change to the way of life of present and future learning communities. Schools should be about improving the life chances of their pupils, as well creating environments in which pupils' inherent abilities can be further developed. The emotional climate of a school has been shown to contribute significantly to that development. How schools adapt their processes to deliver the agendas for extended schools, ECM, healthy schools and the use of the outdoor classroom, while at the same time raising standards, is central to their future success. There is plenty of evidence that this can be done[1]. In a truly sustainable school all these aims are delivered as a package, with sustainability at the core.

Isn't this what education is all about?

You are not alone in this pursuit, no matter what you may think! More and more schools are acting in a sustainable way. Increasingly, school leadership teams wish to be seen to be promoting the concept of sustainability and are developing practices that make visible their commitment to their communities and spread the message.

The need for networks

You can only do a certain amount on your own, and major change will only be achieved by working together with other schools, in networks. "Sustainability" will only have any real meaning when we have extended communities of practice across the whole of the United Kingdom. Then sustainable behaviour may become second nature.

Nevertheless, the journey starts with individual steps, no matter how tentative. The examples of best practice that follow in this chapter should be of considerable assistance in taking these first steps.

These case studies should be understood as particular initiatives from individual schools. They may provide you with ideas that you can replicate in your school, but they are not blueprints for success. Each school and its community has to find its own solution.

Hagbourne CE Primary School, Oxfordshire

A long-term commitment to sustainability

Hagbourne began working on sustainability in the mid-1990s. The management undertook an audit of what they were doing and identified what they wanted to achieve. They made certain that they got the parents, the governors, the staff and, of course, the pupils on board from the outset. Initially they focused on environmental concerns so they turned down the heating, closed doors and windows, instituted a process of turning off lights whenever rooms were vacated, and invested in water-reduction measures.

Eventually pupils got involved in managing the process through the curriculum. Now the evidence of ongoing daily monitoring is made visible to them through computer-linked programs that identify daily electricity, water and gas usage. The data produced is included in subject studies. Physical evidence of the commitment to sustainability is manifest in wind turbines and solar panels to heat the school swimming pool.

The school has an "eco-committee" which directly inputs into school policies, and pupils are given opportunities to explore citizenship in a practical manner by working in their community.

The school reports annually on its environmental progress and is a Green Flag school under the Eco-Schools programme. In 2007 the school was recognized by the National College for School Leadership as a beacon school for supporting other schools in their drive towards sustainability. Its environmental policy identifies how the school will use the environment to develop the skills, knowledge and values required to develop positive and responsible attitudes and develop a global dimension to pupils' thinking.

The school has an Eco-committee which directly inputs into school policies, and pupils are given opportunities to explore citizenship in a practical manner by working in their community. One example of this was a project to redevelop a disused community resource known as Shovel Brook. The school uncovered the area around the brook, cleared it completely, and exposed the spring at its source so that people could see the water coming from the ground. Then pupils established a water meadow, planted native species of trees, put up a bench so that people could sit in the area and admire it, and put up an identification board to show what the school had done and why. It was the school's way of giving something back to the community.

The school has developed international links and uses video-conferencing to maintain and develop those links. The British Council gave it an award for international approaches to its curriculum. The school also raises funds for a wide range of international and local social causes.

Parents are involved in Family Learning days. Local people are encouraged to use the school's facilities and the school provides a weekly lunch for local pensioner groups.

The school has encouraged its pupils to take a positive approach to staying healthy by organizing walking buses and encouraging pupils to cycle to school, and has supported cycling by providing a new storage area for bicycles which is lit by a wind turbine. The school actively encourages parents and staff to share cars.

Pupils are involved in a healthy eating programme and they compost school waste. The school has won awards such as the Volvo Eco Awards for young environmentalists and a water-efficiency award sponsored by Thames Water for its commitment to waste efficiency. Through its pupils it has created and maintained a wildlife area and a sensory garden within the grounds, has planted trees and is tenant of an allotment.

Bowbridge Primary School, Nottinghamshire

Fighting deprivation in the community

Bowbridge Primary School in Newark, Nottinghamshire views itself as a learning community where ESD is at the heart of school improvement. It promotes pupil learning about sustainability through its curriculum, its practices and its community focus.

The school has an "E-team" which promotes energy efficiency throughout the school. It sources local food for its in-house school kitchen, which produces healthy options for its pupils and other members of the community, including parents and family members. Pupils also grow vegetables on the school site, and these are incorporated into school menus.

Pupils generally walk to school and are encouraged to do so with walking buses. The school operates as a local recycling point for paper, aluminium cans and clothes.

The curriculum has a global focus and parents and pupils are encouraged to "think global and act local". The school pursues ethical and sustainable purchasing policies. Sustainability is embedded in the curriculum, specifically in Citizenship education and Social and Emotional Aspects of Learning (SEAL), but also in geography, science, art and other curriculum subjects.

All teachers in the school have signed up to a WWF online course in ESD. ESD is linked to the performance management of the teachers. An ESD action plan for each class and year group embeds ESD into the curriculum. The school is also a Forest School, with year groups attending courses at a local woodland, and a mini-forest school facility has been established in the school grounds, providing valuable curriculum enrichment.

The school has an "E-team" which promotes energy efficiency throughout the school.

The school is currently (2008) involved in a rebuilding programme under the Primary Capital Programme. The school's building charter puts sustainable development principles at the heart of the new build. All materials are to be obtained from a sustainable or renewable source. All materials used will be ethically produced and where appropriate, such as in the playgrounds, recycled materials will be used, while building materials will, where possible, be sourced from local suppliers to reduce the carbon footprint of the build. Waste materials will be kept to a minimum and where appropriate materials will be recycled on site. The builders will be locally based and encouraged to minimize transport miles in the construction process. The site will be environmentally managed. In addition, contractors will be expected to keep the local community informed about progress and adherence to the agreed code.

Since 2001 Bowbridge has led a series of initiatives to improve the health, economic well-being and environment of local people. It has done this by providing a wide range of extended services, which are focused on the community it serves. For example, the school discovered that a combination of low income and lack of energy efficiency in homes contributed to high levels of fuel poverty in the community. The school talked with pupils about their use of energy and water, and their views about efficiency and waste. Practical measures were suggested to save money and reduce the environmental impact. The energy and water initiative was popular with pupils and highly effective at conveying the message to families. It has been extended to all local residents, in partnership with a local energy advice agency.

The school has established a community cafe, a community library, a crèche for parents, and high-level quality care for pupils before and after school hours. Recycled ICT equipment is available for parents who might not be able to afford to buy new. Parenting classes link to the work being done by pupils in school, so that parents can play a more effective role in their children's education. These are provided free.

This Nottinghamshire primary school at the heart of the local community works to fight poverty and deprivation, not in spite of its practical commitment to sustainability, but because it sees sustainability as benefiting the community.

Crispin School, Somerset

Making global citizens

Crispin is a Leading Edge secondary school with a specialist responsibility in ESD, global education, Assessment for Learning and teacher training. The school believes that action-based learning should be provided to deliver on the ESD agenda, and that it has a responsibility to provide students with the knowledge and understanding to prepare them for a sustainable future. The school was awarded the DCSF Award for Sustainable Schools in the West of England at the 2007 Teaching Awards. WWF, Unesco and the DCSF have all acknowledged its achievements, and the school features in a CD about sustainable development produced by WWF.

The Deputy Headteacher has overall responsibility for ESD, but all the staff are charged with implementation. The school has developed a number of environmental project areas, such as a courtyard garden to provide space for quiet contemplation, developed with the aid of Learning Through Landscapes. A green committee of staff and governors, which meets half-termly, is responsible for maintaining environmental standards on the site and in the curriculum. The school aims to be a Fair Trade school and seeks to source food items in an ethical manner. A "Green Code of Practice" is posted throughout the buildings. The many recycling initiatives it has launched since 1990 include paper collection from local residents and recycling of aluminum cans on the site and from the community. The School has Green Flag status from the Eco Schools programme.

The school provides curriculum days focused on sustainability so as to enhance staff and student understanding of the issues.

The school believes its students should be global citizens by providing international links and supporting a number of charities that operate in the developing world. It has links with schools in Kenya, and provides enhanced curriculum opportunities to address issues of global sustainability.

The school curriculum takes a broad approach to sustainability. In art it is delivered be designing areas of the school grounds with an environmental theme. In design and technology the focus is on design with minimal environmental impact. Environmental sustainability is examined throughout the geography curriculum. Mathematics uses environmental data in the understanding of spreadsheet analysis and statistical analysis. PSHE looks at worldwide issues that focus on sustainability. Opportunities are available in RE for exploring "humankind and the environment". Programmes such as "grow it, cook it and eat it" help students to develop understanding about sustainable approaches to food production and consumption. Finally, the school provides curriculum days focused on sustainability so as to enhance staff and student understanding of the issues. During these whole sections of the school are involved in activities that promote sustainable development, global education, waste management, environmental management and biodiversity.

A woodland area, planted and maintained by students, has been developed on the school site, while a pond, wildlife garden and nature trail provide learning opportunities. A specialist green room gets its energy from alternative sources such as wind, sun and solar-heated water, while solar-powered data-logging equipment is used in science on environmental projects. Students have been involved in the design of a sustainable redevelopment programme to be undertaken on the school site.

The governors have formally agreed that any future building will be sustainable.

In developing its agenda Crispin School works with a range of national organizations, including WWF, the Royal Society for the Protection of Birds, the British Council and Learning Through Landscapes. The school's aim is for students to leave with a sense of global responsibility and an excellent understanding of sustainability issues for the future.

As science teacher David Heath puts it, "The children embrace sustainability, which gives them a certain confidence. If you asked any one of them to deliver a speech about fair trade or recycling, they'd be able to."

Cassop Primary School, County Durham

Using carbon-neutral technology

Winner of the first National Sustainable Schools Award at the 2007 Teaching Awards ceremony, Cassop Primary School has over a considerable period of time worked to integrate education for sustainable development in all of its work. The teachers, governors and the site manager have all played significant roles in the development of sustainability at the school, under the leadership of headteacher Jim McManners.

The school displays and uses all forms of renewable energy – biomass, wind, and solar. It is powered by carbon-neutral technology in the form of a 50kW wind turbine and is heated by a biomass boiler which uses locally sourced recycled wood waste and locally grown willow. The hot water in the school is produced by solar panels, while photovoltaic cells contribute to the energy supply.

Pupils learn about sustainability by making connections between their actions and the quality of their environment. Thus they can make and test wind turbines and photovoltaic cells, and pupils visit local landfill sites to learn about recycling and waste reduction as well as energy production from waste. They undertake environmental investigations both on site and in local environments such as Cassop Vale nature reserve.

The school uses the school environment and its local surroundings as a source of inspiration and learning for pupils – for example, pupils learn about butterfly conservation and carbon-neutral energy production from studying the area around the school. Low-energy light bulbs are in use throughout the school and elected pupils, known as energy monitors, graph and analyse the school's energy and water use to identify opportunities for reduction.

Cassop has links with five schools in Europe and one in Kenya, sharing information and ideas on energy and the environment.

Cassop School aims to be the centre of its community and has taken steps to open its doors to others through its commitment to the local environment. Courses are run for other schools and for adult groups in the school's environmental sustainability centre, allowing them to make use of the school's facilities and encouraging all to become more knowledgeable and enthusiastic about environmental issues. The school's wind turbine project involved a community consultation by the pupils which produced a 98 per cent positive response.

Courses are run for other schools and for adult groups in the school's environmental sustainability centre, allowing them to make use of the school's facilities and encouraging all to become more knowledgeable and enthusiastic about environmental issues.

In 2007 Cassop was recognized as an outstanding school by Ofsted, which said that pupils had "excellent understanding as to how to lead healthy lives" while "their contribution to the local and wider community is outstanding". The headteacher believes that there is a direct link between its performance and the fact that children learn by working on projects which are rooted in the real world rather than artificially constructed in the classroom.

Developing the vision for this school was not something that was created overnight: getting to focus on sustainability has taken time and stamina. But it has shown that a small school can work beyond its boundaries with other schools, organizations and with industry.

Canon Burrows CE Primary School, Greater Manchester

Fostering a green environment in an urban area

Despite being situated in an urban area and on a busy main road, Canon Burrows School, in the Waterloo area of Ashton-under-Lyne, has a variety of well-maintained gardens, landscaped areas and playing fields.

A key part of this is a nature reserve which the school has established in part of the valley of Taunton Brook, which lies within the school grounds. For over 20 years children from the school have been working on Taunton Brook, to maintain and improve the environment for the benefit of the whole community. The school gained its first Eco-Schools Green Flag in 1998 in recognition of its ecological strategy and whole school approach to sustainability, and has now gained permanent Eco school status.

This dedication to care for the environment is at the core of the school's ethos. Children, teachers and a variety of adult helpers at the school have planted trees, shrubs and flowers, and have created pathways, bridges and viewpoints in the school grounds. Each week a group of children go outside and work on projects in a structured programme of environmental education. As well as the weekly work, Canon Burrows has whole-school action days, in which all pupils are involved in such things as painting murals on school mobile classrooms, planting trees and bulbs and an annual spring clean of the local environment.

The school achieved beacon status for its focus on education for sustainable development, and works with other schools on developing sustainability as an element of school improvement. Ofsted recognized its environmental education work as a strength and said that the programme at the school "enriches the curriculum and has a significant positive impact on pupils' personal development, knowledge and understanding".

A dedicated sustainable development co-ordinator has their own management budget and the backing of the senior leadership team. The ESD co-coordinator monitors ESD work in the curriculum, conducts termly reviews and present reports to governors with recommendations for aims to include in the school development plan.

The practical work on Taunton Brook is not just an add-on activity. The school explicitly aims to embed sustainable development in the curriculum, highlighting its relevance to each subject and cross-referencing across the curriculum. The school grounds are fully used as a teaching resource. Paper, aluminium cans and clothing are collected from the community and recycled, and waste vegetable matter is composted. The school has developed a healthy school programme and children grow vegetables for consumption in school.

The global focus in the curriculum areas is enhanced by links to schools in Europe and in helping develop a global dimension in Initial Teacher Education programmes.

A dedicated sustainable development co-ordinator has their own management budget and the backing of the senior leadership team.

The school's original Eco committee was merged into the School Council in 2006, which now leads on the subject of sustainability. The pupils monitor electricity, gas and water consumption, and the data collected is used in classroom learning. Pupils are encouraged to walk to school through a walking bus scheme and staff at the school are encouraged to share cars.

Involvement of pupils in the sustainability agenda has had a significant impact on both pupil performance and behaviour. In 2005 Ofsted identified "very well behaved pupils, who have very good attitudes to learning, are enterprising and very keen to take on extra responsibilities ... A stimulating learning environment, enhanced by an innovative, creative and inclusive curriculum. The school focus on the environment and the excellent outdoor facilities both in the grounds and the nature trail make a significant contribution to pupils' understanding in science."

The school seeks to work with its wider community through management of the nature reserve for community use, participating in Tidy Days in the local community, and working with external organizations such as Groundwork Trust.

As it says in the school's prospectus, the aim of Education for Sustainable Development at Canon Burrows is: "to give pupils a greater understanding of both natural and human systems through a range of immediate environmental experiences which engage their senses, emotions, and thinking. It should enable pupils to develop a life ethic which values all people and the natural environment, and to become aware of the actions that they ought to pursue in order to live more a more sustainable life both now and in the future."

St Christopher's School, Wrexham

Improving pupils' self-confidence

St Christopher's School is the largest special school in Wales with 225 pupils. It caters for pupils with wide and diverse special educational needs including moderate and severe learning difficulties.

The school has a strong commitment to sustainability and has permanent Eco School status. The environmental/ sustainability work of the school was driven by its deputy headteacher, Chris Pittaway, who had a particular interest in developing pupil skills through active participation in community-based projects. He aimed to develop the skills needed to participate fully in the community through a variety of programmes, including the school's Eco-Centre.

The school has constructed a sensory garden, allotments, a Japanese garden, and Greek/Roman garden. It helped lead a local 14 to 19 Learning Pathways initiative via its curriculum enrichment programme. Citizenship skills are developed through community environmental work. The pupils have ownership of the school grounds and are actively engaged in practical environmental work. Paper, old computers, ink cartridges, cardboard, metal, wood, florescent tubes and bark mulch are recycled regularly.

Led by Chris Pittaway, in 1998 pupils from the school set up the Millennium Eco Centre at nearby Borras Quarry. The aim was to raise awareness within Wrexham County Borough's schools and the wider community of the importance of recycling and waste management issues, and in general to develop knowledge of the impact of a more sustainable lifestyle. The centre is a collaboration with the quarry's owner, Tarmac. The school's own recycling takes place here.

Special significance is given to waste minimization and global citizenship activities for pupils at St Christopher's and for all schools that attend the Centre's regular programme of courses on sustainable development.

Tarmac and St Christopher's have further plans for Borras Quarry.

Extensive native tree planting is taking place, with pupils planting the trees needed to transform the site into a park. In September 2007 an award of £80,000 was made by the Aggregates Levy Sustainability Fund to continue its environmental work with the community. Each of the centre users are encouraged to develop an awareness and new skills in environmental issues.

The aim was to raise awareness within Wrexham County Borough's schools and the wider community of the importance of recycling and waste management issues, and in general to develop knowledge of the impact of a more sustainable lifestyle.

Learning is accredited with Open College Network units in environmental skills, and pupils can gain Millennium Volunteer hours for supporting the environmental activities pursued at the Eco Centre site.

St Christopher's initially introduced ESD into the curriculum to develop in pupils a clear understanding of the world they lived in and to give them a sense of place. Making sustainability a cornerstone of their development has increased the pupils' self confidence and sense of identity. Pupils, even those with profound learning difficulties, help run the Eco Centre, developing planning, leadership and organization skills as well as practical environmental skills and enhanced research skills.

The Long Eaton School, Derbyshire

A science college promoting sustainability on all fronts

The Long Eaton School is a specialist science college of 1,268 pupils aged between 11 and 19. It has a long tradition of concern for the environment, consistently highlighting awareness of environmental issues through the school's vision statement, the curriculum, assemblies, Science College Development Plan, special enrichment events and representation at national and international events. The school aims to live its motto, "Opening doors to the future".

An Eco committee meets twice a term, and is open to pupils, teachers, local Groundwork Trust representatives, the county Eco-Schools co-ordinator, and the site manager. Each year group in the school has a student council which links directly into it.

The school takes a shared responsibility approach to its sustainable development work, with teaching staff, the head of environmental studies, head of PSHE, and the Citizenship coordinator all co-operating to promote it. Parents are told of the school's commitment to the environment when they apply for places for their children, while the school vision underlines its responsibilities:

Care and respect for ourselves, others and the environment.

Co-operation between school, home and community.

According to the School Food Policy, all food and drink offered to pupils, staff and visitors should be nutritionally healthy and, where possible, produced locally. This approach won Long Eaton Healthy School Status and a regional teaching award.

The design of the school buildings deliberately encourages efficiency in the use of energy and water. Their use is continually monitored by the school site manager, with assistance from pupils. Harvested rain water is used to flush the toilets.

As part of their Citizenship course pupils have instigated schemes for recycling plastics and bottles, while paper, cardboard and cans are reused or and recycled wherever possible. There is a policy of only printing when necessary. Equipment and lights are switched off when not in use and as far as possible the school reuses or disposes of old equipment in an environmentally sound way

The Travel Plan promotes walking and cycling to school. The school engages with BSM Cycling projects and Derbyshire County Council's "Travel Smart" scheme to encourage the promotion of walking and cycling to school. Consistently high numbers of pupils cycle and walk to school – on average 1100 of the 1268 each day.

The school buildings have been specifically designed to encourage efficiency in the use of energy and water, which is continually monitored by the school site manager, with assistance from pupils.

The school has worked with the Derbyshire Wildlife Trust to develop green open spaces on the campus and used recycled materials to build outdoor furniture. One of the outcomes from this was that the school was asked to be part of the Growing School Garden at Hampton Court Palace Garden Show, where they won a Silver Gilt Award. The school has also developed vegetable gardens, tackled the thorny issue of sustainable school meals and lobbied for a bridge over a local canal to make it easier for pupils to cycle to school. At the heart of a new school building is an enviro-lab that includes a science lab and a garden area. The latter serves as a learning zone and home to an after-school gardening club, while crops, such as cabbage and leeks, are used in the school's healthy meals.

Participation in activities to link the school to the wider world includes: the International Tulip Project, which maps climate change across the northern hemisphere; working with Rotary International to fund the building of deep bore wells in Tanzania, West Africa and India; recycling all of its toners through an offset scheme run by Ricoh UK which plants trees in Africa; and forging curriculum links with schools in other countries. Pupils have represented the UK at United Nations Children's Conferences, speaking on environmental issues.

The policy for sustainability forms part of the school improvement plan, and is reviewed annually by the senior leadership team and governing body. All curriculum teams monitor progress towards the school's sustainability objectives.

The school works to promote the profile of sustainability more widely by organizing an annual conference with other schools and local business organizations.

Ofsted identified Long Eaton as an extremely effective school, offering excellent value for money. "Many students make a highly effective contribution to school life and the wider community, for instance through work on the school council or promoting the conservation activities of the 'eco club'" (Ofsted report, 2006).

Kingsmead Primary School, Cheshire

A collaborative approach

Kingsmead is the first school in Cheshire to have been designed and built on the principles of sustainability and consideration for the environment.

The timber for the building's glulam (a laminated and glued timber frame, made from recycled timber) structural frame was sourced from sustainable sources, as was the external timber cladding. The roof structure is inverted to provide for rainwater capture for use in toilets and urinals. Walls and roof were insulated to a significantly high level so that the school outperforms the requirements of the 2002 UK building regulations. A biomass boiler fuelled by locally produced wood chip from waste timber powers the heating system. The roof has both photovoltaics to provide electricity and a solar panel array to provide hot water. The building provides flexible spaces for different styles of teaching, and the classrooms run across its northern aspect to provide consistent light without overheating in summer.

A DfES study in March 2006 emphasized the value of a collaborative attitude to sustainability at all levels: "A further vital factor is the attitude of the school governors and teachers to the project. At Kingsmead, everyone embraces a wholehearted approach to environmental responsibility, led by the head and staff, but also communicated simply and clearly to all who use the building – children, parents and visitors alike." The study said it had "not found a better case where the energy-efficiency making 'make performance visible' has been put into practice".

The school is committed to healthy eating with balanced options and a school tuck shop that provides healthy snacks. Parents are told on the school website what healthy choices are available each week and by email on a Friday of the actual healthy choices their children have consumed in school.

The school was built as an exemplar in sustainability by Cheshire County Council, but not all aspects of the design have been been entirely successful, notably the biomass boiler system has not functioned as was hoped. But the county council has accepted that fine tuning the operational capability of such a structure will take time to achieve. Many of the sustainable features built into the school in 2004 could now be used in future builds without incurring the same high costs. By and large the building provides an excellent working environment, and it is expected that utility and maintenance costs will be up to 50 per cent less than those of the previous structure.

The National Audit Office was emphatic in its support: "By focusing during its design and construction on the whole-life value that Kingsmead Primary School could deliver, Cheshire County Council has delivered a building that provides a high-quality teaching and learning environment with comparatively low running costs. By working closely together at an early stage the client and its delivery partners were able to establish a clear shared objective of delivering a school that would operate to high environmental standards and provide an environment in which teachers and pupils could thrive."[2]

The site has a vegetable garden for pupils and each classroom has an uninterrupted view of green space. Pupil recycling officers ensure that all paper waste is recycled. The school has winter gardens – unheated buffer zones between classrooms and the playground, used for wet play and to minimize heat loss from the school. There are also two outdoor classrooms and a butterfly garden. Wherever possible planning and resource materials are stored on the school network, rather than in paper form.

The school is committed to healthy eating, with balanced options and a school tuck shop that provides healthy snacks. Parents are told on the school website what healthy choices are available each week and by email on a Friday of the actual healthy choices their children have consumed in school. The school is committed to Fair Trade processes, buying Fair Trade products when possible. Both pupils and parents are encouraged to walk or cycle to school.

The staff at Kingsmead take a cross curricular approach to teaching and learning to reflect the agenda of a Sustainable School for the 21st century. Much of the work is topic-based and the pupils started one year with a topic entitled "Our Building and

Our Environment". In 2008 the school gained an Eco-Schools Green Flag.

The curriculum is based on knowledge and understanding of global sustainability. This is developed through science, geography and history. PSHE and Citizenship education focus on enabling pupils to be active participants in their own learning and become independent learners. Children are given opportunities to undertake outdoor and adventure activities through residential visits. The environmental workings of the building are on view, and incorporated into history lessons and science lessons. Laptops in the classroom show how conditions are being maintained and rainwater trickles through transparent pipes in the corridor. The school is developing a wildlife pond, for use as an outdoor classroom. The school also runs a Royal Horticultural Society (RHS) gardening club and has achieved RHS gold medal status for its work.

The school's commitment to wider community involvement is apparent in its efforts with local groups, businesses and services, including environmental groups and faith communities, to enhance outcomes for children while ensuring respect for the diversity and valuing the contributions of all. The school acts as a community recycling point to collect waste materials on behalf of the Woodland Trust. The Kingsmead Family Association regularly surveys the local community to gauge opinions on the use of school facilities by the community.

The school has an elected school council to represent pupil voice in the school. There is also an elected Eco group which includes a governor and a member of the teaching staff, and which leads the environmental agenda in the school. Parents are encouraged to walk or cycle with their children to the school.

Kingsmead was designed from the beginning as a sustainable school. However, the sustainability of any school is dependent upon the way in which it operates and the principles by which it lives. Kingsmead exemplifies how this can be done.

Seaton Primary School, Devon

Committed to using renewable energy

"Caring now for the future" is the motto at Seaton Primary School, in East Devon, where every child planted a tree in the grounds when it first opened 25 years ago.

More recently a range of renewable energy technologies have been installed, including a 4.7kW PV array of solar panels which supplies electricity to the school, reducing the school's CO_2 emissions by 2 tonnes per annum, a wind turbine and 48m^2 of solar water heating panels for the school's outdoor swimming pool. The school has been awarded the prestigious Ashden Award for Sustainable energy use.

The renewable energy technologies installed by the school provide outstanding learning opportunities for the pupils. Seeing renewable energy in action in their own school stimulates the pupils' interest in energy issues. Pupils in the Eco Club and class Energy Agents help to reduce energy wastage by ensuring lights and equipment are switched off when not required and doors and windows are closed to prevent heat loss. Members of the after-school Eco Club assist the Energy Agents and report their observations to the Student Council and at assemblies. The Eco Club, together with teachers, governors and the caretaker, forms an Energy Task Force which monitors the use of energy in the school, reviews practice and suggests and implements improvements where possible. Pupils are encouraged take the message home and become ambassadors for change in society.

There are regular reviews of the curriculum to identify opportunities to incorporate sustainability.

Parental support is sought in promoting cycling and walking to school. The school organizes cycling proficiency training and incorporates cycling into the school curriculum.

An area of the school grounds is reserved for composting. There is a substantial woodland and an orchard has been planned to provide fruit for pupils while offsetting some of the school's carbon emissions. Currently the school is installing a large grey-water collection system to re-fill the school wildlife pond and to demonstrate small-scale water power.

The school is also committed to ensuring that any new building or refurbishment work incorporates the highest specifications for sustainable construction. For example, it is exploring installing a ground source heat pump in a proposed new classroom block.

There are regular reviews of the curriculum to identify opportunities to incorporate sustainability. This has, for example, produced initiatives to examine weather, climate change and global warming, and a range of teaching materials on energy efficiency developed with Rolls Royce apprentices for use by other schools. These are available on the school's website (www.seatonprimary.co.uk).

The school is committed to reducing its waste output by 50 per cent and ensuring that all pupils and staff have the knowledge to incorporate sustainable waste management practices in their own lives, both inside and outside school. The school has undertaken waste audits and the information given to pupils to enable them to plan reduction strategies. Pupils have organized recycling schemes in school to collect plastic and cardboard.

Seaton School has been awarded Healthy School status because of its emphasis on providing regular exercise, encouraging healthy eating and the drinking of water. In 2006 Ofsted judged that "Pupils have an exceptionally good understanding of the benefits of adopting a healthy lifestyle".

Community resources are utilized to extend the school curriculum and through links with organizations in the local and wider community, for example Natural Watt, a renewable energy company, provides live updates on the school's energy turbine performance. (Information on the school's performance from renewable energy can be viewed at http://www.naturalwatt.com/Education/SeatonDashboard/tabid/179/Default.aspx.) As the school is a member of the Sustainable Axe Valley Enterprises (SAVE) Trail, local people can visit it so see working exemplars of sustainability.

Raglan Primary School, Bromley

Spreading the message about the environment

Raglan Primary School is a foundation school of 410 children. Education for Sustainable Development is not only embedded in the school curriculum but is also a central focus in all the school's activities. The school has a subject manager for environmental education who has responsibility for developing the "real curriculum" and for setting annual targets for environmental education in the school's improvement planning. The school has been an Eco School since 1996 and now has permanent Eco School status (2003). It is committed to spreading the message about sustainability, to the extent that it has created an inspiring road show which has trekked around other schools – infant, junior and even secondary. The school has also developed Raglan in Bloom days when its gardens are open to former pupils and the wider community. Litter in the community was addressed by adopting a local street.

There are three focuses in the curriculum:

survival – keeping healthy, keeping safe and skills for life

sustainable development – recycling, safer transport, global greed and the redistribution of wealth

citizenship – being happy, local and national government and world projects.

The school has created an inspiring road show which has trekked around other schools – infant, junior and even secondary.

The school has a scheme of work for environmental education, while sustainability is mapped into schemes of work for all subjects. The school's commitment to ESD has been recognized by Ofsted as making a significant contribution to its overall work. Specific days that address a global approach to the curriculum underline the school's positive international outlook, and it has established links with schools in India and Bermuda.

Pupils are involved in planning environmental changes for the school. Years 5 and 6 each have their own Eco Club. In addition an Eco committee, consisting of governors, teachers, classroom assistants and other interested parties, addresses environmental issues in the school.

This school has an unstinting commitment to recycling and waste minimization. Its wide range of recycling projects include foil, cans, inkjet cartridges, paper, shoes, glass and water filters. The school participates in the Woodland Trust Christmas Card recycling scheme and has collected many hundreds of thousands of cards from the community. Pupils collect waste materials on site for recycling and composting. The school has an ethical and green purchasing policy which includes recycling paper.

Five established garden areas provide different environments for use in a range of curriculum subjects. The school site is maintained by pupils acting as "Green Rangers" who keep it free of litter.

> "A strong emphasis on environmental education pervades almost all aspects of the school's work and gives it a distinctive character ... The curriculum is greatly enriched by environmental education ... Curriculum breadth is added particularly by environmental education ... Pupils' spiritual, moral, social and cultural development is outstanding. They learn about the importance of looking after each other and their environment." Ofsted

References

1   UK Panel for Education for Sustainable Development, 1998, DEFRA
2   *Improving Public Services through Better Construction,* National Audit Office, 2005

7 Teaching and Learning for Sustainability

The National Curriculum already provides significant opportunities for developing understanding among pupils and students of sustainable development across all Key Stages and beyond, and in most, if not all, subjects. It is a matter for curriculum leaders and managers to identify where those opportunities exist, while governors should be asking questions about how they are achieving the objectives. While it is not possible here to provide detailed guidance on all the opportunities in the curriculum, this chapter aims to give an overview and pointers as to how learning

Note for governors

As a governor you should have an oversight of the delivery of the curriculum in your school. If you have a particular subject, curriculum area or key-stage responsibility you have an opportunity to enquire about how sustainable development is covered. In addition, the governing body as a whole could decide to evaluate the place of ESD overall. It might be that the governing body asks that all curriculum policies include some statement about ESD so that students will be asked to consider the environmental, social and resource implications of the materials that they use.

It is legitimate for governors to enquire about how the curriculum is being delivered. This chapter should help you ask appropriate questions of your headteacher or other senior managers.

about sustainability can be delivered across the normal range of subjects taught. Suggestions are given for how sustainability issues can be used or introduced in different units and topics of the curriculum.

Curriculum subjects

The study of texts from different cultures and traditions in **English** broadens global understanding and can enable students to discuss and interact on ESD issues. In writing assignments students can address issues of poverty, health and differential life chances that occur across the world and communicate views on those through a variety of media.

In **Mathematics** ESD can be addressed by using relevant data, e.g. covering carbon footprinting, global travel, quality-of-life indicators and the interpretation of social statistics.

Science provides opportunities for understanding sustainable development through developing skills in decision-making, exploring values and ethics in the applications of science and technology, and enhancing students' knowledge and understanding of the key concepts of diversity and interdependence.

Geography has a major role in developing ESD at all Key Stages, by fostering an understanding of key concepts, developing critical enquiry, and giving students the ability to handle complex information while exploring attitudes to the use of resources and globalization, and associated questions about values.

History provides opportunities for ESD through developing the skills of enquiry, critical thinking and communication. It also provides knowledge and understanding of how actions, choices and values may impact on future societies and their economies and environments.

Design and Technology nurtures skills in creative problem-solving and thinking and evaluation, develops knowledge and understanding about the principles of sustainable design, and explores values and ethics in both the design and manufacture of goods.

Citizenship provides ESD opportunities by developing pupils' skills, commitment and participation in democratic decision-making processes. This can be done through a focus on the quality, structure and health of the environment and exploring the values that society places upon this process.

ESD can feature in **Art and Design** through giving students an understanding of their role in creating sustainable environments, as well as exploring the values and ethics expressed through them.

Physical Education should be used to promote ESD through explaining and encouraging healthy lifestyles as well as providing students with opportunities for developing decision-making skills.

ICT can enable students to link with other schools around the world, comparing views on sustainability. Pupils could learn about modelling by using energy-monitoring software on their own ICT systems. The Globe programme provides help with collecting and using statistical data on the environment.

Modern Foreign Languages provide opportunities for linking with other schools across the world to analyse differences in lifestyles. Internationally important issues such as climate change can be explored through direct contact with pupils in countries already feeling the impact of them.

Leisure, Travel and Tourism courses provide significant opportunities for students to examine issues of sustainable tourism, including the impact on local populations of developing air travel and carbon outputs.

The **Every Child Matters** agenda calls for all children to be healthy, safe, able to enjoy and achieve, make a positive contribution and achieve economic well-being – all of which correspond exactly to the goals of ESD.

Note

In the lists in this chapter titles in bold refer to the Programmes of Study for each subject and their subsections, e.g. "Geographical enquiry skills, 1C", or, for some subjects, to the non-statutory guidelines. "Units" refer to the sections in the associated Schemes of Work.

Early Years Foundation Stage

The statutory guidance for the new Early Years Foundation Stage curriculum in England identifies opportunities for learning about sustainable development in the section on Knowledge and Understanding of the World.[1]

The programme calls for children to be given activities that provide first-hand experience of problem-solving, prediction, decision-making and discussion through exploration and observation. These activities should be presented in learning environments that stimulate children's interest and experience, including out of doors.

Children can be encouraged to learn about plants and animals through planting schemes and sensory trails, as well as investigating materials and objects through observation. They can explore the range of materials used in the school itself and discuss their origins and the sustainability of using such materials. They could demonstrate care and respect for others, living things and their environment through activities such as growing and caring for plants or the careful use of materials.

Creative activities, such as experimenting with natural sounds and materials, can develop children's vocabulary and communication skills, but it is important to let the learning develop through play.

Mathematical awareness can be developed at this age by measuring the growth of plants and using natural materials to look at shape and size.

Healthy eating can be encouraged from a young age by growing vegetables which are then used in school foods.

Key Stage 1

Science
SC2, Life processes and living things,
Living things in their environment,
Variation and classification 4a: similarities and differences between themselves and others and to treat others with sensitivity.

5c: exploration of care of the environment.

Geography
Geographical enquiry and skills, 1c: expression of views about people, places and the environment, where they can discuss local themes such as litter.

Knowledge and understanding of places, 3c: how places have become the way they are and how they are changing.

Knowledge and understanding of environmental change and sustainable development, 5a: recognition of changes in the environment such as traffic pollution in a street.

5b: recognition of how the environment might be improved and sustained by restricting the use of cars.

Breadth of Study, 7a: a study at local scale.

7b: fieldwork outside the classroom.

History
Knowledge and understanding of events, people and changes in the past, 2a and **2b:** why people did things and what has happened as a result; identification of significant differences between ways of life at different times in history.

Breadth of study, 6a: changes in pupils' own lives and the way of life of their family or others around them.

Key Stage 1 (cont.)

Design and Technology

Knowledge and understanding of materials and their components, 4a: the working qualities of materials, which can include looking at sustainability, recycling and waste.

Unit 1D, Homes: the principles of environmental sustainability in features of buildings such as double-glazing, insulation, gardens, the use of local materials.

Unit 1B, Playgrounds: the use of materials including recycling.

Unit 1C, Eat more fruit and vegetables: the origins of fruit and vegetables, seasonality and transport issues.

Citizenship

Unit 3, Animals and Us: the introduction of rights and responsibilities as well as understanding about basic human needs.

Unit 5, Living in a diverse world: people's identities, communities and different places in the world; how other people and living things adapt and survive in their environments; links to the science curriculum.

Unit 7, Children's rights – human rights: the promotion of equality as well as respect and care for others.

Art and Design

Evaluating and developing work, 3a: evaluation of the work of other cultures through discussion. **3b:** through discussion identification of how pupils might change their current work in the light of increasing evaluation.

Knowledge and Understanding, 4b: exploration of the materials pupils are using linked to sustainability.

4c: exploration and examination of the work of other cultures and periods.

Physical Education
Unit 19, Outdoor and adventurous activities: enhancement of trail activities by developing elements that focus on acquiring information on the biodiversity of the environment in which pupils are working; work on co-operative problem-solving tasks; discussion of the importance of the outdoor environment to healthy lifestyles.

ICT
Unit 2C, Finding information: use of a CD-ROM encyclopedia to research habitats or specific environments which are directly related to ESD criteria.

Key Stage 2

Science
Unit 2B, Plants and animals in the local environment: learning about plants and animals in their immediate environment and how differences between places result in a different range of plants and animals being found; could include descriptive evaluation of local habitats and understanding about growing conditions.

Unit 5/6H: investigative work around an environmental question.

SC2, Life processes and living things, Living things in their environment: opportunities for developing an understanding of environmental concerns and of the need to maintain biodiversity at a local and international level.

Geography
Geographical enquiry skills, 1c: expression of views about people, places and environments; could be linked to **Unit 8, Improving the environment,** which encourages pupils to investigate local environmental issues and develop plans to address them as well as becoming actively involved in the process; links to reduction in consumption, reuse, recycling and waste.

5a and b: knowledge and understanding of environmental change and sustainable development, recognising how change in the environment can be achieved and how communities seek to manage their environments sustainably through local projects; could link to **Unit 17, Global eye,** and a focus on recycling in the community.

Breadth of Study: local fieldwork studies for understanding of local environmental issues such as traffic and pollution.

Mathematics

MA4, Handling data: consideration of the energy and water used in the school by analysing spreadsheets of usage data or identifying food miles associated with food consumed in school.

Design and Technology

Knowledge, skills and understanding and evaluating processes and products: Recognition that the quality of a product depends on how well it is made and how well it meets social, economic and environmental considerations.

Unit 3A, Packaging: evaluation of the sustainability of product design, material usage and the packaging and the processes associated with product development; questioning the environmental impacts of materials.

ICT

Exchanging and sharing information: sharing and exchanging information in a range of forms through international links, enabling pupils to understand the views and perceptions of young people from around the world.

Breadth of Study: exploring information from a variety of sources so as to gain broader understanding of the ways in which information is used (also **Unit 6D, Using the internet to search large databases and to interpret information**)

Key Stage 2 (cont.)

Citizenship

Developing confidence and responsibility, 2J: different ways resources can be allocated and how choices affect individuals, communities and the environment; how the energy requirement of a community might be reduced through the development of greater understanding of the impact of carbon outputs in the production and management of energy.

Unit 6, Developing our school grounds: redevelopment of the school site with a school garden, improving play spaces, or creating space for wildlife in the school grounds.

Developing a healthy, safer lifestyle, 3a: what constitutes a healthy lifestyle including the benefits of healthy eating choices and the importance of exercise to a sustainable lifestyle; link to knowledge of fitness and health and why physical activity is good for health and well being.

Key Stage 3

Science

Sc2, Life processes and living things: protection of the environment and the importance of sustainable development.

Unit 7C, Environment and feeding relationships: understanding of environmental variation and change and the impact this has on plants and animals.

Unit 9G, Environmental chemistry: climate and environmental change and the importance of evaluating data to understand the impact of global warming.

SC3, Materials and their properties: developing an understanding of the impact of burning fossil fuels on the environment and how these might be mitigated.

SC4, Physical processes, Energy resources: the variety of energy resource and the distinction between renewable and non-renewable resources; various means of generating electricity.

Unit 7I, Energy resources: the importance of renewable energy and the impact of fossil fuel burning.

Unit 9I, Energy and electricity: how energy gets wasted.

Breadth of Study, 1c: the benefits and drawbacks of scientific and technological developments, including those related to the environment, health and quality of life.

Unit 9M, Investigating scientific questions: evaluation of scientific enquiry as it is related to ESD, such as in examining global warming; the benefits and drawbacks of scientific and technological developments, including those related to the environment, health and quality of life.

Key Stage 3 (cont.)

Design and Technology
Evaluating processes and products: identification how the quality of products is judged, including whether they meet clear fit-for-purpose criteria, the appropriate use of resources, and the environmental impact of their production.

Units 9A, Selecting materials and B, Designing for markets: opportunities to develop an understanding of process and production and the impact such processes and production have on global sustainability.

Geography
Geographical enquiry and skills, 1e: appreciation of how people's values and attitudes, including their own, affect contemporary social, environmental, economic and political issues; clarification and development of pupil's own values and attitudes about such issues.

Unit 12, Images of a country: understanding of places by questioning initial impressions of a country.

Unit 20, Comparing countries: exploring perceptions of selected countries and developing skills of independent geographical enquiry.

Knowledge and understanding of environmental change and sustainable development, 5a: description and explanation of environmental changes such as deforestation and recognition of ways of managing such processes.

5b: exploration of the idea of sustainable development and recognition of its implications for people, places and environments and for students' own lives.

Unit 14, Can the Earth cope?: topical issues about sustainability and the environment.

Art and Design

Breadth of study, 5D: art, craft and design in the locality, in a variety of genres, styles and traditions, and from a range of historical, social and cultural contexts.

Unit 9C, Personal space, public places: exploration of examples of public art in students' local area; research into the different ways in which ideas, beliefs and values are represented and shared in their local area and in different times and cultures, including contemporary practice; using a range of media, ideas and concepts about sustainability, seeking to provide environmental protection and global citizenship.

Citizenship

Developing skills of enquiry and communication, 2a: looking at topical political, spiritual, moral, social and cultural issues, problems and events through analysis of information and its sources, including ICT-based sources.

Unit 10, Debating a global issue: with focus on the Amazonian rainforest, enhancement of students' knowledge and understanding of environmental change and issues of sustainability.

Religious education

Unit 7E, What are we doing to the environment?: the approaches of different religions to issues of conservation and stewardship; exploration of the implications for the world of unrestrained consumption.

Key Stage 4

Science

SC2, Life process and Living things, Living things in their environment, 5b: how the impact of human beings on the environment depends on social and economic factors including population, industrial processes and levels of consumption and the production of waste; the science behind genetically modified organisms and their possible impacts.

5c: the economics and societal and environmental impact of agribusiness.

SC4 Physical processes, Energy resources and energy transfer, 5b: the efficient use of energy, the need for economical use of energy resources, the environmental implications of generating energy from fossil fuels, the economic importance of resource depletion and the impact on climate change.

Breadth of Study, 1c: the benefits and drawbacks of scientific and technological developments, including those related to the environment, personal health and quality of life, and those raising ethical issues.

Design and Technology

Developing, planning and communicating ideas, 1b: issues that affect planning, for example, the needs and values of different users, moral, economic, social, cultural and environmental considerations.

Evaluating processes and products, 3c: ensuring that products are of a suitable quality for intended users, meeting a range of considerations such as moral, cultural and environmental; modifications that would improve their performance if necessary. Students should be able to develop their own criteria for evaluating the cost and benefits to a society in economic and development terms of resource efficiency processes.

ICT
Reviewing, modifying and evaluating work as it progresses, 4b: the impact of ICT on students' own and others' lives, considering the social, economic, political, legal, ethical and moral issues; consideration of how ICT could contribute to sustainable development by, for example, reducing travel and consumption patterns.

Citizenship
Knowledge and understanding about becoming informed citizens, 1j: issues of global interdependence and responsibility including Local Agenda 21 and sustainable development, and participation in the political process.

Unit 9, Consumer rights and responsibilities: the ways in which consumer choice can impact upon sustainable development across the world.

Unit 12, Global Issues Local Action: exploration of local responses to global issues such as sustainable development, and how decisions can impact on quality of life issues and the future environment.

Business studies
The changing business environment: Introducing business: the economic, social and environmental aims of and constraints on businesses; the environmental regulation of business through issues of air, water, noise pollution and the importance of resource efficiency as well as the social effects of changes in the business environment; the role of sustainable development in business objectives and decisions and the growth of corporate social responsibility reporting.

Key Stage 4 (cont.)

Geography: Sustainable Development opportunities and Geography GCSE

The requirement to teach sustainable development as part of GCSE geography varies across the examination boards.

A number of units of study, such as "People and the Environment", "Places and People", "Economic Development" and "Managing Natural Resources", provide opportunities to identify the ways in which climate influences environments, human activity and social development. This includes the need for a focus on sustainable development, and an understanding of the impact of human activity on natural ecosystems such as the relation between economic activity and climate change as well as the global threats posed by unrestrained economic development.

The opportunity for achieving sustainable development, through conservation, resource substitution, recycling, pollution control and the use of renewable energy as well as the need for stewardship, conservation and the growth of green tourism, and the importance of fair trade to global citizenship is extremely important in understanding sustainability.

GCSE programmes identify opportunities to study the impact of a sustainability focus in areas such as changes in cities and towns, the urban-rural push-pull effect, social welfare, and economic drivers for sustainable use of resources.

People and the environment: the ways in which climate influences environments and human activity and societal development, including the need for a focus on sustainable development: understanding the impact of human activity on natural eco-systems; the economic consequence of the sustainable management, of forests and of human activity; the importance of sustainable management of eco-systems, and their international impact; economic activity and its impact on climate change; global threats posed by unrestrained economic development.

Managing natural resources: social, economic, environmental and political issues and consequences of increased resource use, especially those that are non-renewable; achieving sustainable development, through conservation, resource substitution, recycling, pollution control and the use of renewable energy; the need for stewardship and conservation and the growth of green tourism; the importance of fair trade to global citizenship; the impact of resource depletion and scarcity of resources; the importance of resource recycling for sustainability strategies; the global threat posed by resource depletion.

Economic development: the possible environmental impact of transport policy; the impact of economic activity on society; the conflict between, economic development and environmental issues; the importance of economic development, as part of sustainable development, as well as the societal impact of environment damage and wealth creation; how society can contribute to sustainable development policy; the global threats posed by economic development; strategic management of tourism.

Maintaining food and water supply: environmental and human determinants of food and water supplies and the impact they have on human life; the role of national and international agencies and the security of food and water supplies.

Urban and rural links: the impact of push-pull factors in environmental terms; the consequences of migration on society and on the individual; the management of green belt strategies and the impact of these on housing; the impact of development strategies on worldwide migration patterns; understanding the role of governments in managing change and migration.

Every Child Matters

The Every Child Matters agenda can be delivered with a focus on sustainable development. Sustainable development is about helping pupils develop knowledge and understanding, as well as acquiring the appropriate values and skills through learning experiences, that are key to effective sustainable development understanding.

The National Curriculum, in 1999, made clear that "ESD enables people to develop the knowledge, values and skills to participate in decisions about the way that we do things individually and collectively, both locally and globally, that will improve the quality of life now without damaging the planet for the future."

References

1   *Statutory Framework for the Early Years Foundation Stage,* DCSF 2007, ref. 00013-2007BKT-EN

8 Helping You Achieve Your Sustainable School

At the time of writing over 7000 schools have signed up to the Eco-Schools programme. This is an international scheme, developed in 1994 by member organizations of the Foundation for Environmental Education (FEE), supported by the European Commission. It aims to raise issues of environmental and sustainable development among school students across the world by encouraging them to participate in a range of practical activities that reduce their school's environmental impact. Schools that have made substantial efforts to improve their environmental performance gain an award.

The UK government has indicated that it would like all schools to become Eco-Schools. But putting sustainability at the centre of their school's culture is clearly a challenge for many school leadership teams and governing bodies.

Research in 2007 by the *Times Educational Supplement* and the Consortium (education suppliers) found that 72 per cent of a sample of 300 headteachers had not heard of the *National Framework for Sustainable Schools*, which is central to the DCSF's agenda for green schools! Seventy-nine per cent were making no effort to discover their school's carbon footprint and fewer than 30 per cent had actually undertaken even simple efforts to make their schools more sustainable. Few schools had sought to provide school meals from locally sourced materials and less than 30 per cent were making any effort to change students' travel habits.

But the journey to sustainability does not have to be a lonely and difficult path. There is a considerable amount of support available from government, NGOs and business organisations. This chapter identifies actions schools can take and the main sources of guidance.

The National Framework for Sustainable Schools

The key government document for developing sustainable schools in the UK is the DCSF's *National Framework for Sustainable Schools*. This consists of a series of eight "doorways", which identify the main issues to be addressed by a sustainable school. The framework is supported by a number of tools and advice guides that are available on the sustainable schools website at http://www.teachernet.gov.uk/sustainableschools/index.cfm. The eight doorways are designed to help schools put sustainability at the heart of their business.

The government has set national targets to be achieved by 2020, which include:

a 20 per cent reduction in greenhouse gas emissions (from 1990 levels)

a 30 per cent reduction in greenhouse gas emissions when there is an international climate agreement

renewable energy generation to meet 20 per cent of all energy consumption

---

The Eight Doorways

Travel and traffic

Food and drink

Energy and water

Purchasing and waste

Buildings and grounds

The global dimension

Promoting inclusion and participation

Local well-being

a reduction by 2020 of 16 per cent from 2005 levels in UK greenhouse gas emissions from sectors not covered by the EU Emissions Trading Scheme

10 per cent of fuels used for road transport to come from renewable sources, subject to their being produced in a sustainable way.

In 2006 the government also set a series of clear targets for reducing carbon dioxide emissions in the UK: a 60 per cent reduction of CO_2 output by 2050 compared to 1990 levels and a 26 to 32 per cent reduction by 2020. Schools are expected to play their part in achieving these targets, which the government wants to be legally binding.

The Climate Change Bill, which was introduced into the House of Commons in November 2007, states that progress towards these targets must be reported upon by all government departments, and that the government must report to Parliament their assessment of the carbon risk to the UK. Included in the Bill is a system of five-year carbon budgets which will set binding limits on CO_2 emissions, backed by independent scrutiny.

As part of the process towards reducing the carbon footprint of the government estate some 68 national indicators have been developed. Government departments are expected to move towards carbon neutrality and all new schools are expected to become carbon-neutral by 2016. Schools which are being rebuilt under the Building Schools for the Future programme are expected to reduce their carbon emissions by 60 per cent through improved building design, for which additional funding of £50 per square metre has been allocated.

The eight doorways or themes are not in themselves new to schools, but they do give school leaders and governors the opportunity to examine how their school may introduce or develop its focus on sustainable development. The approach behind the doorways is that there is a significant connection between what children learn and the actions of a school. Thus schools should be seen to be modelling sustainable behaviour to students and to the wider community.

The doorways are metaphors for ways of approaching the challenges faced by schools. Each one suggests routes to getting to grips with these through the school curriculum, the management of the school site and the school's connections with the wider community. They thus provide an opportunity for schools to address broader global issues while at the same time tackling particular issues within their own context. The framework has been written so that leadership teams can map onto it much of what they do already.

The Eight Doorways and how to use them

Travel and traffic

Ensure that the school has developed a school travel plan which addresses the issue of student safety and sustainability. Governors should monitor its implementation. Funding of up to £10,000 is available to improve travel to and from school including the provision of cycle facilities. The plan should feed into the school development/improvement plan.

Reduce the numbers of car journeys to and from school.

Reduce the number of car-parking spaces on the site.

Provide opportunities through the travel plan for increasing numbers of students to walk or cycle to school, with safe and secure facilities for students to store their bicycles, and offer road-safety education as a part of the curriculum.

In the primary sector encourage walking buses.

As a last resort, for those whose children cannot walk, cycle or use public transport to school, encourage car-sharing.

Guidance on travel and traffic

Guidance on school travel planning can be found on

http://www.teachernet.gov.uk/wholeschool/sd/managers/travel/STAtoolkit/stp/

at http://www.dft.gov.uk/pgr/sustainable/schooltravel/

Your local authority will have a school travel adviser; consult them for help in administering the travel plan.

Governing bodies could delegate an interested governor to take responsibility for this agenda and where appropriate challenge the school management teams about its delivery.

Food and drink

Government advice is for food to be prepared on site, with a lot of it supplied locally.

Ensure that in supplier contracts freshness and quality of food and drink supplied to students are clearly specified.

Guidance on food and drink

Advice for schools is available from the DCSF on developing sustainable food policies, while the DCSF and DEFRA have produced a public-sector advice toolkit on food procurement which can be found at

http://www.defra.gov.uk/farm/policy/sustain/procurement/pdf/initiative-outline.pdf

http://www.DfES.gov.uk/valueformoney/index.cfm?action=Good Practice.Default&ContentID=21.

http://foodinschools.datacenta.uk.net/

The Schools Food Trust has been set up to help schools deliver this agenda. It provides independent support and advice for schools. It can be found at

http://www.schoolfoodtrust.org.uk/index.asp

The Food in Schools programme, which is a joint venture between the Department for Health and the DCSF, sets out to encourage schools to take a whole-school approach to healthy eating and gives advice and support on

http://www.foodinschools.org/

The Food Standards Agency and National Governors' Association joint publication *Food Policy in Schools* (2005) gives guidance to governing bodies on promoting healthy eating.

Ensure that the school is promoting the Healthy Eating agenda to its parents and the wider community.

The National Healthy Schools programme should be an integral part of the strategy for improving food and drink in the school. Local community organizers and teams of education and healthcare professionals are available to help deliver the agenda.

The governing body should have policies in place to address nutrition, sustainability and food procurement as well as providing opportunities for students and their parents to learn about healthier eating.

Incorporate programmes such as Growing Schools from the DCSF and the 2007 Year of Farming and Food in the school curriculum.

Offer training to school catering staff on how to provide healthy, nutritious and sustainably sourced meals.

Address the issues of healthy and sustainable food procurement in the school development/improvement plan and report progress regularly to the governing body.

Energy and water

Include energy management in development planning.

Gather information about energy consumption and use this when considering investments in plant and technology.

Provide training for all staff, teaching and non-teaching, in managing the use of energy.

The increasing use of school premises under the extended schools agenda requires that significant thought by the leadership team should be given to the introduction of energy-saving measures and the zonal development of heating plant.

Regular maintenance schedules are crucial to efficient use of energy plant.

Produce clear policy documents on energy and water conservation.

Governors should monitor the implementation of these policies.

Ensure the curriculum provides pupils with the knowledge to make effective conservation decisions in their own homes and in their communities.

Transmit the message on water and energy conservation to the wider community through describing the school's processes and practices in written communications.

Consider "Thin Client" solutions (see chapter 3) when buying ICT equipment. It has been reckoned that these can reduce energy costs by as much as 89 per cent and reduce CO_2 emissions by as much as 78 per cent in schools.

Invest in water-saving measures such as push taps, reduced-capacity cisterns, push systems on showers.

Monitor water usage weekly.

Fit infra-red controllers on urinals.

Avoid buying ICT equipment that needs air conditioning in the rooms where it is sited.

Monitor the performance of ICT equipment regularly as ICT accounts for 5 per cent of a school's energy consumption.

Guidance on energy and water

Support available to the school includes schemes of energy and water certification for schools through the DCSF and technical assistance from water companies to ensure schools comply with water regulations when installing new equipment.

The Low Carbon Buildings Programme, which can be found at http://www.lowcarbonbuildingsphase2.org.uk/page.jsp?id=2, provides advice and financial support for schools to install micro-generation equipment as well as photovoltaic power, solar power, wind turbines, ground-source heat pumps, bio-fuel boilers and CHP (Combined Heat and Power) plant.

The DCSF's Capital Assets team gives advice on the design and management of school facilities, at

http://www.teachernet.gov.uk/management/resourcesfinanceand building/schoolbuildings/

Purchasing and waste

Conduct life-cycle analyses of the products and services used.

Set performance targets based on a life-cycle analysis and minimization of waste.

Governors should monitor how procurement and waste management strategies are being carried out.

Ensure purchasing decisions are influenced by environmental standards and by information about eventual upgrading.

Look to upgrade and repair equipment, including ICT, where possible rather than automatically replacing it.

Ensure that the curriculum is cultivating the attitudes, knowledge and skills needed to address sustainable consumption and waste.

Source links with the community to promote the messages of sustainable consumption and waste minimization.

Set challenging targets for consumption and waste reduction. Make the targets public and report annually on progress.

Guidance on purchasing and waste

The Sustainable Development Commission's website provides a lot of advice:

> http://www.sustainable-development.gov.uk/government/
> task-forces/procurement/index.htm

The DCSF's Value for Money Unit provides excellent guidance for schools on making informed choices and effective use of school resources, at

> http://www.dcsf.gov.uk/valueformoney/index.cfm?action=Good
> Practice.Default&ContentID=21

Buildings and grounds

Develop school grounds so as to enable pupils to learn about the natural environment and sustainable management of land.

The management of the school environment, built and natural, should provide the local community with access to and understanding of sustainable design principles, and the link between sustainable design and human well-being.

Set ambitious targets to reduce the carbon footprint of the school and increase the environmental performance of the buildings and grounds.

Examine how the school buildings, grounds and the management of them contributes to student understanding of sustainability.

Through oversight of the awarding of contracts and service provision ensure the promotion of excellence in environmental awareness and sustainable procurement in the school's wider community.

The BSF Programme offers unparalleled opportunities for transforming school design and grounds. Governors should work with the school community, local authority officers and design and build organizations in ensuring that school buildings and grounds are designed, built and managed in such a way as to significantly reduce their environmental impact.

Guidance on buildings and grounds

There are many tools on the Sustainable Schools website, which can be found at

www.teachernet.gov.uk/sustainableschools

These can support the understanding of sustainability in general in schools, and include design guides and case studies.

The global dimension
The curriculum should provide opportunities for students to be prepared to live their lives in a global community with an understanding of sustainable development, interdependence and social justice.

Priorities for school leaders are set out in the DCSF's *Putting the*

World into World Class Education: an international strategy (see below).

The success or otherwise of inculcating an international perspective in pupils should be reported in the SEF.

Consider creating a global citizenship policy that ensures the school's commitment to sustainable principles are enshrined in a global outlook.

Guidance on the global dimension

Support for the development of a global dimension is available to schools through the DCSF International School Award and through curriculum enrichment materials from the Department for International Development, details of which can be found at

http://www.globaldimension.org.uk/

The Development Education Association and Teachers in Development Education (TIDE) provide considerable resources to promote the international agenda, including teacher visits. The Development Education Association can be located at

www.dea.org.uk

and TIDE at

http://www.tidec.org

Global Gateway, Oxfam and the British Council sites all provide information and linking opportunities for schools and students to develop an international dimension to their work:

http://www.globalgateway.org.uk

http://publications.oxfam.org.uk/oxfam/resources.asp

http://www.britishcouncil.org

The DCSF strategy for world/ global education can be found in the Department's programme *Putting the World into World-class Education: an international strategy* (2004). This identifies three overarching goals with associated priority actions. Details can be found at

http://www.globalgateway.org.uk/Default.aspx?page=624

Governors can challenge the school to provide evidence of a global dimension in its curriculum and social activities, through the management of its estate and through its links with schools in the United Kingdom and abroad.

Provide CPD on how to address the global dimension for staff where necessary.

Promoting inclusion and participation

Sustainable development can only be achieved with improved social equity and social progress, according to the World Commission on Environment and Development in the Brundtland report of 1987, *Our Common Future*. Local community cohesion to some extent depends upon the ability of us all to develop a capacity to value difference and diversity, and to develop respect, care and understanding. Thus sustainable development requires acceptance of social inclusion and equality.

Get involved with the local and wider community through Education Improvement Partnerships (EIPs – local collaborations of learning providers, careers services, trade unions, employers and faith groups) so as to improve outcomes for young people by seeking to improve educational performance, attendance and the personalization of student learning. Improvement for all is at the heart of the EIP process, while collaboration is one of the keys.

Ensure the curriculum addresses issues of diversity and injustice.

Encourage students to participate in school decision-making through student councils.

Participate actively in the development of the Children and Young People's Plan in your community through engagement with the local authority.

Encourage young people to become involved in local sustainability projects through organizations such as the Federation for Community Development Learning or Peace Child International.

Develop school policies on accessibility, race relations and special educational needs that refer to sustainability as a complementary target.

Ensure that all relevant school contracts promote the principles of sustainability, inclusion, and a respect for diversity.

Get the school to focus on working with its community to identify people's feelings about inclusion, and develop policies and actions that address cultural diversity and the school community's participation in decision-making processes.

Guidance on promoting inclusion and participation

Details on promoting inclusion and participation can be found at the Qualification and Curriculum Authority on

http://www.qca.org.uk/qca_6402.aspx

The Sensory Trust provides materials on creating inclusive environments, and can be found at

http://www.sensorytrust.org.uk

Education Partnership approaches can be found at

http://www.standards.DfES.gov.uk/sie/si/eips/

or at

http://www.teachernet.gov.uk/management/atoz/e/eip/

Your local authority should have details of local education improvement partnerships or look at the Every Child Matters Plan agenda in your local area. National guidance details can be found at

http://www.everychildmatters.gov.uk/strategy/planningandcommissioning/cypp/?asset=document&id=28094

Local well-being

Developing their grounds gives schools opportunities to forge links with their communities. The extended schools agenda provides the perfect vehicle for students to do this. Moreover, getting involved with development projects that are designed to enhance the lives of the local community empowers pupils and substantially raises their confidence levels. It also provides them with experience of the decision-making processes in society.

Aim to establish your school as a hub of the community, not just for learning but also as a source of support, by providing opportunities for local community groups to hire meeting rooms, providing space within the school for local community organizations, developing crèche and nursery facilities, and encouraging local support groups.

It is an essential aspect of a sustainable school that it is engaged with its wider users and regularly involves them in identifying the community's development needs and the role of life-long learning in helping individuals realize their personal ambitions. It is very easy for school to become inward-looking, so there is a

Guidance on local well being

Bowbridge Primary School in Newark, Nottinghamshire (see chapter 6) is an example of a school that has had a significant impact on its wider adult community and has come to be seen as the hub of regeneration in the local community:

http://www.bowbridgeprimary.com

Further information on local well-being programmes can be sourced through the Sustainable Development Commission website at

http://www.sustainabledevelopment.gov.uk/progress/national/68.htm

The Every Child Matters Agenda as addressed by schools through the extended school initiative can be found at

http://www.everychildmatters.gov.uk/ete/extendedschools/

Information may also be obtained from regional government offices throughout England.

The national Healthy Schools initiative contributes to local well-being, and local Primary Care Trusts work with local authorities to manage the Healthy School programme. Information on this can be sourced at

http://www.wiredforhealth.gov.uk/cat.php?catid=842

Information on developing quality living spaces can be sourced through

http://www.cleanersafergreener.gov.uk

role for governors in reminding the leadership of this agenda. Local well-being may be the most appropriate of the eight doorways to be addressed as a whole-school approach.

Sources of guidance on becoming a sustainable school

Strategic, Challenging and Accountable: a governor's guide to sustainable schools, DfES, 2007

This toolkit for governors discusses the contributions and responsibilities they can make to promoting sustainability. It identifies that there is no single way to becoming a sustainable school and that schools need to focus for themselves on their own way of moving forward. It includes the outline of a two-hour workshop which governors can work through, and offers governing bodies a series of activities to help them think about and plan for the development of a sustainable school. It identifies learning outcomes and helps governors take the national framework forward. See:

http://publications.teachernet.gov.uk

Chronos for Schools

A software tool developed by Cambridge University Programme for Industry (CPI). It is an e-learning tool which enables participants to step into the shoes of a headteacher seeking to use the sustainable schools agenda to deliver the ECM programme. It provides access to case studies of schools that have followed a sustainability path. It can be used as for stand-alone e-learning.

Learning Pathways, WWF

A tool that contains a set of activities to help schools develop a whole-school approach to sustainability. The activities in the programme require participation by all members of the school community involved in the development, design and planning of Learning for Sustainability programmes. It allows participants to upload their outcomes onto a website so as to share their experiences with other schools. The programme includes output of a school action plan to help the school become more sustainable. It can be accessed as a pdf file as well on the DCSF's Sustainable Schools website at:

http://www.teachernet.gov.uk/sustainableschools/wwftool/

Further details can be accessed from WWF learning at:

http://www.wwflearning.org.uk/wwflearning-home/
pathwaystochange/pathways/

Planning a Sustainable School: driving school improvement through sustainable development, DCSF, 2008

Guidance for leadership teams, staff and governors that provides a number of participatory activities intended to help schools plan, implement, monitor and evaluate their progress towards becoming a sustainable school. It emphasises the importance of planning and links to national strategies and the Sustainable Schools Self-Evaluation Tool. See:

http://publications.teachernet.gov.uk

The Sustainable Schools Self-Evaluation Tool

Known as s3, this can be accessed through the DCSF's Sustainable Schools website. It focuses on a whole-school self-evaluation of the progress being made towards sustainability. The school can document its efforts and report on the improvements and benefits that have accrued as a result. The headings are the same as in the 2005 Ofsted self-evaluation framework, thus assisting schools to write evaluative statements about their progress. The tool can be found online at:

http://matrix.ncsl.org.uk/GMATRIX_2168836_19606681/11
94795665484/rebrand/matrix/index.cfm?matrix=125&force
new=yes

or as a pdf and Word document at

http://www.teachernet.gov.uk/sustainableschools/tools/tools_
detail.cfm?id=2

School Grounds Evaluation Tool – Measuring Success

From Learning Through Landscapes, the school grounds charity, this toolkit is aimed at schools and school grounds managers. The pack includes an introduction to evaluation concepts, a range of activities for students and adults on evaluation, a video and a set of questionnaires for pupils and staff. It is designed to take schools through the process of improving their school grounds from initial enthusiasm to a final evaluation of the outputs. Details can be found at:

http://www.ltl.org.uk/schools_and_settings/resources/publications.htm?subject=39&searchsub=1&ms_type=&mssearch.x=33&mssearch.y=0&item=383

The School Works Toolkit

This kit was developed for the School Works charity to enable schools to undertake a participatory approach to the design of new schools. It identifies how to set up a participatory process step by step, from the questions that might be asked to the techniques available. The school works approach has been shown to have wide-ranging and tangible benefits by involving young people in the design of their local environment, which includes, of course, building a new school. The programme was designed as a partnership between school-design professionals, educationalists and schools. It enables schools to define their project, decide who will be involved in it, create a project team, develop a questioning approach, and develop a plan for the project. It provides techniques and exercises to promote debate linked to the curriculum experience of students, enables schools to design workshops and collate the design brief, and suggests opportunities for evaluating the process and its outcomes. Finally, it shows how to put together a competitive process for choosing an architect for the programme, how to appoint contractors and how to monitor the building process.

The toolkit can be sourced from School Works as a free downloadable pdf at:

http://www.school-works.org/publications.asp

Work at Waste in School, from Waste Watch

A tool designed to help schools evaluate and audit waste, and to implement practical ideas to tackle it. It includes case studies from schools across the UK, data on the volumes of waste produced in UK schools, and two packs, "Dustbin" and "Wise up to Waste", intended to develop practical learning experiences for pupils. The programme can be used to spread the message into the wider community. See:

http://www.wastewatch.org.uk/Education-and-Training/At-School

Think Leadership

A free online tool from Heads, Teachers and Industry Ltd, a not-for-profit organization working at the interface between industry and education. The tool, which was developed with support from Severn Trent plc, provides the opportunity for schools to benchmark their environmental performance against similar schools. The site contains Asset Management Plan data from 25,000+ schools in England, Scotland, Northern Ireland and Wales. It allows schools to benchmark their performance in terms of energy, water usage, waste and recycling, biodiversity, air quality and pupil activities, as well as to gain access to information about sustainability. Schools get an action plan produced for them which they can upload into a school improvement/development plan, and can update the Asset Management Plan data held on the site once they have registered.

The tool can be accessed at:

www.thinkleadership.org.uk

and further information and support can be obtained from Heads, Teachers and Industry Ltd, Herald Court, University of Warwick Science Park, Coventry CV4 7EZ

Communications toolkit, DCSF

This is designed to help explain the aims of the sustainable schools strategy and encourage parents, teachers and the community to become involved with the programme. It provides access to pupil materials such as the School Carbon Detectives' kit – a package for Key Stage 2 and 3 students to investigate the sustainability performance of their own school – and resources for teachers and school leaders on how to profile sustainable development in school assemblies. The resource library features sustainability in Schemes of Work and links to National Curriculum subjects. There is a *Governors' Handbook* on sustainable schools and a *Bursar's Guide*, both of which give practical guidance on placing sustainability at the heart of the school development agenda.

The site also provides access to a number of useful web resources:

http://www.teachernet.gov.uk/sustainableschools/tools/tools_d etail.cfm?id=11

Action at School, from Global Action Plan

An environmental programme designed to help schools save money and reduce their impact on resources. It links to the Key Stage 3 and 4 curriculum. The programme lasts three terms and is designed to help schools tackle waste, water usage, energy usage and transport. Global Action Plan will train an action team in the school to measure their school's environmental impact and build effective partnerships with local community organizations in the process. Usually it requires third-party funding.

Details about the programme can be found at:

http://www.globalactionplan.org.uk/schools.aspx

Schools and Sustainability – A Climate for Change, Ofsted

In the process of undertaking this evaluation inspectors visited a selection of primary and secondary schools to assess teaching about sustainability and progress towards meeting the expectations of the National Framework for Sustainable Schools.

The report, published in 2008, identifies that in the best lessons teachers use a range of imaginative activities to help pupils develop and test out their views on complex ethical issues.

However, most of the schools visited had limited knowledge of sustainability, and work in this area tended to be uncoordinated, often confined to special events rather than being integral part of the curriculum.

The reports offers governors and school leaders the means to evaluate their own school performance in the light of outcomes. It should provide a challenging focus for any school that wishes to become sustainable.

Awards

To help schools make progress there are various award schemes, each of which focuses on specific goals. Note that these are the ones available at the time of writing, and that they can change, be withdrawn or replaced at any time

1. Green Schools

The award is run by the Young People's Trust for the Environment (YPTE) on behalf of the oil company Total. The aim of the awards is to stimulate interest in young people aged 7 to 11 in environmental issues, either through research or projects located in their schools. The awards are designed to encourage cross-curricular work on the environment, and they link in with the National Curriculum at Key Stage 2 in England and Wales and the 5-14 Scottish Curriculum. Their aim is to create interest in all forms of energy, including fossil fuels and alternative technologies.

There are four different award categories. Schools may enter group projects into one or more of them. Category winners receive cash prizes for the school.

Totally Powered Up

Projects in the "Totally Powered Up" category should focus on energy and making use of an energy source. For example, in terms of the curriculum this could be research on different energy sources, global warming, and energy and the environment, or designing environmentally friendly lighting systems, or designing a solar-powered car. The project could be applied to science, technology, geography or citizenship.

Totally Active
These projects should involve work within the school grounds, such as starting and tending vegetable plots, or a project that uses waste materials from the school.

Totally Clued Up
This category allows for curriculum-wide projects that research any aspect of the environment. For example, in English it could be a project on an environmental aspect of a foreign country such as global warming, flooding, fishing and hunting, or agriculture.

Totally Creative
The "Totally Creative" category is for art, music and poetry projects on environmental themes, such as works of art or music that use recycled materials.

Details of the Green Schools Award can be obtained from:

> Young People's Trust for the Environment, 3a Market Square, Crewkerne, Somerset, TA18 7LE; tel. 01460 249 163
> http://ypte.org.uk/docs/greenschoolawards/

2. The International School Award
The International School Award (ISA) is an accreditation scheme for curriculum-based international work in schools. The programme has three levels (foundation, intermediate and full) and can be used with pupils aged five to 18. It is managed by the British Council on behalf of the DCSF.

The award is designed to involve and develop the wider community of the school, as well as providing a framework to form and develop international links. It encourages and supports schools to develop the following:

an international ethos throughout the school

a majority of pupils within the school impacted by and involved in international work

collaborative curriculum-based work with a number of partner schools

curriculum-based work across a range of subjects

year-round international activity

involvement of the wider community.

Ideas are provided for developing collaborative curriculum-based work with partner schools across the world.

The programme seeks to develop a whole-school curriculum approach to issues such as culture, poverty, pollution, recycling, food, music and sustainability. The International Schools Award materials can be found at:

http://www.globalgateway.org.uk/default.aspx?page=1343

or

http://www.globalgateway.org.uk/default.aspx?page=2915

3. Eco Schools

This programme was developed after the 1992 Rio Summit by the Foundation for Environmental Education. Today it is delivered in more than 40 countries worldwide.

The Eco Schools programme is free and assists schools in tackling sustainability issues. Schools follow a simple seven-step process which helps them to address a variety of environmental themes. They are required to address such topics as litter, waste, energy use, water use, transport, healthy living and a global perspective. The programme, which leads to a prestigious European environmental award, shows that the school is committed to achieving the highest standards in environmental education and management. It involves at the minimal level setting up an action team that includes pupils, conducting an environmental survey, and drawing up and implementing an action plan.

Pupils are expected to lead on this programme. They are required to form an Eco committee and through consultation with the rest of the school and the wider community decide which environmental themes they want to address and how. Schools work towards gaining one of three awards – Bronze, Silver and the prestigious Green Flag award, which symbolises excellence in the field of environmental activity. Bronze and Silver are both self-accredited via the Eco Schools website, while the Green Flag award is externally assessed by the environmental charity ENCAMS. Grants are available to help pay the costs of attaining the Green Flag.

ECO Schools Award scheme can be accessed at:

Internationally	http://www.eco-schools.org
England	http://www.eco-schools.org.uk
Scotland	http://www.eco-schoolsscotland.org/home/index.asp?linkID=6
Wales	http://www.eco-schoolswales.org
Northern Ireland	http://www.tidynorthernireland.org/eco-schools/index.php

4. Rights Respecting Schools

This UNICEF programme focuses on promoting the United Nations Convention on the Rights of the Child (UNCRC).

The aim of the award is to encourage schools to teach effectively about human and children's rights, including rights and respect in all aspects of relationships between teachers, adults and pupils. The school is expected to embed the values of the UNCRC in its curriculum and ethos. Regional support is available to advise schools on the award scheme.

To achieve the award schools are required to achieve a specific standard in four aspects of how they promote children's rights:

leadership and management, in embedding the values of the UNCRC in the life of the school

knowledge and understanding of the UNCRC

rights respecting classrooms

pupil participation in decision-making throughout the school.

Each topic is designed to contribute to the development of an active global citizen. The award is meant to link into Eco Schools and the Healthy Schools Award.

Rights Respecting Schools Award can be accessed at:

http://www.unicef.org.uk/tz/teacher_support/rrs_award.asp

5. The Royal Society for the Protection of Birds

The Royal Society for the Protection of Birds (RSPB) runs two award schemes, both of which are mainly targeted at under-13s:

Wildlife Action Award

Climate Action Award.

These awards do not have to be achieved through schools, they can also be gained by children in clubs (including an extended school club) or by individuals.

The awards identify practical activities that are designed to benefit the climate and wildlife.

The Wildlife Action Award involves completing 28 tasks and the Climate Action Award six tasks out of a possible 11. The awards are given at three levels (Bronze, Silver and Gold), depending on the number of tasks that have been successfully completed.

The schemes can be accessed at:

http://www.rspb.org.uk/youth/join_in/climate/index.asp

http://www.rspb.org.uk/youth/makeanddo/do/actionawards/index.asp

6. Sustainable Learning

This is a free programme that provides advice and support to schools wishing to improve their environmental sustainability by reducing their energy and water bills. Sustainable Learning is managed by CREATE (Centre for Research Education and Training in Energy) and BRE (Building Research Establishment).

The focus of the award programme, as it stands at present, is only on sustainable energy and water management.

7. The Ashden Awards

These awards are supported by the Sainsbury's Charitable Foundation. The Ashden Award for sustainable energy is an annual competition to identify and reward truly excellent, practical and innovative schemes. They are open to different businesses and projects from across the world, and include an award on sustainable energy just for schools.

This school award offers a first prize of £15,000 and second prize of £5,000 and is open to any UK school with pupils aged between five and 16. The school needs to have created a sustainability ethos in which responsible use and generation of energy is a key component.

Information about the awards and links to a sustainable energy knowledge centre can be found at:

http://www.ashdenawards.org

8. Healthy Schools

The National Healthy Schools Programme is a long-term initiative that helps young people and their schools to be healthy. It supports the links between health, behaviour and achievement with the aim of helping children and young people to be happy and healthy and to do well. This is a national programme run jointly by the national Healthy Schools programme and the DCSF.

The programme encourages schools to assess their performance and then to assess themselves again to establish whether there have been improvements. There are four core themes:

1. personal, social and health education (this includes sex and relationships education and drug education)

2. healthy eating

3. physical activity

4. emotional health and well being.

The four core themes link to the school curriculum and the emotional and physical learning environment. There are criteria for each theme that schools need to meet to achieve National Healthy School Status. Although each theme covers a different area, they are all delivered through a whole-school approach. See:

http://www.healthyschools.gov.uk

Index